Table of Contents

Korea Reimagined
An Exploration of Science, Technology, and Medicine

Introduction

Hyeok Hweon Kang
Washington University in St. Louis
May 2022

What do science, technology, and medicine mean from Korea? In this inaugural volume of *WashU Ventures in Korean Studies*, the authors set out to answer the question which has underpinned the rise of new interests within Korean studies: science studies, history of technology, and medical humanities. The essays here range across a wide array of topics, from sedge craft and traditional medicine to mental health, electricity, and kimchi refrigerators. Yet they cohere around investigating the relationship between Korean society and the central human activities of knowing nature, making things, and healing bodies. To better understand contemporary Korea as well as its process of modernization, this volume presents three themes: innovation as method and history, healing and medical identity, and the dialectics of global and local technologies.

The volume opens by examining what innovation means as both a method for writing history and as history itself. First, Campbell Stuart and Sheilly Moreno meditate on hands-on reconstruction as methodological innovation. Stuart reworks a Korean sedge mat and engages the experimental history of science. Moreno then investigates movable type-founding and reflects on both the past and present of artisanal literacies and tacit knowledge. Taken together, their works show that in experimenting with the materiality of the subject matter—though without direct access to the knowledge of the craftspeople and through shortcuts and substitutions—we begin to understand the material imaginaries of historical craft practices.

Yet experimentation had a history of its own, and Gunwoo Lee shows it by tracing the "entangled history of the Korean semiconductor industry." Rather than a simple transfer of knowledge, the rise of semiconductors in the Korean technological landscape had to do with the interplay of imitation and innovation, centers and peripheries, research and production. Whereas Lee focuses on semiconductors, Tony finds innovation within pseudoscience—i.e., the practice of divination in contemporary South Korea. In explaining the continuing relevance and popularity of divination, he emphasizes its "competitive and innovative niche market," which has provided alternative (as opposed to modern scientific) responses to contemporary societal concerns.

The next three essays examine medicine and identity formation. Chloe Sachs traces the history of mental illness and its treatment in twentieth-century Korea. She shows the making of what she calls "hybridized traditional and modern understanding of mental health"—an amalgam of shamanism, Confucianism and Western psychiatry. This, she argues, shaped social stigmas against seeking treatment. Both Ashley Lee and Leah Ford then investigate the histories of traditional medicine and medicinal commodities in the colonial period (1910–1945). Lee intervenes against the "one sided narrative of medical modernization": rather than transitioning seamlessly from Eastern to Western medicine, colonial Koreans in fact preferred the former, a phenomenon she explains by examining the history of medical consumption. Ford continues the story of consumption yet by focusing on the rise of ginseng as a global commodity and marker of "Korean" identity during the colonial period. After tracing the history of Korean ginseng, she demonstrates the critical role of the Government-General of Korea and private Japanese companies in the formation of a vibrant ginseng market which persists to the present day.

The third and last section emphasizes the dialectics between global technology and Korean society. Yael Shaw begins by situating electricity in the global technology circuit, including its formations in China, Japan, Europe, and the United States. Her essay then examines the relationship between electricity and Korean culture, surveying its evolution from the *kaehwa* movement in the nineteenth century to the modern-day Korean Electric Power Company. If electricity shaped culture, the technology of the tracking shot—or camera dolly—transformed cinematography, argues Leandra Djomo. There has been a recent rise in Korean sci-fi films (or speculative media in general), and the Korean zombie genre in particular has attained global popularity: by analyzing its aesthetics and technology, Djomo uncovers the nontrivial role that the dolly played in materializing the strategy of "glocalization."

The last two papers examine domestic technologies. In her examination of kimchi fridges, Nataleya Slade charts the emergence of this distinctively "Korean" technology in the second half of the twentieth century. Slade engages the scholarship on the "social construction of (imported) technology": instead of technical, operational difference, the fridge model that succeeded availed itself of a more favorable economic and social context. Similarly, Paulina Joo investigates domestic work and its automation through a case study of the laundry machine. The social life of this machine goes far beyond the common wisdom that it "liberated" women. Emphasizing its gradual adoption and spread in Korean society, Joo shows that the uptake of the laundry machine was determined by social and economic factors such as the pace of industrialization, changes in the female employment and average domestic work hours, and the patriarchal system.

Taken together, these essays contribute to the emerging field of the history of Korean science, technology, and medicine. They show, with novel perspectives and diverse case studies, that ways of knowing, making, and healing were both agents and objects in the formation of Korean society.

Weaving Together Past and Present: *Wanch'o* and Empirical Reconstruction in Korea

Campbell Stuart

Abstract

Wanch'o products were practical, everyday items that could be made from readily available materials and these items were prized possessions of all social classes dating back to the Silla period (57 BCE – 935 CE). Every step of the *wanch'o* production process requires immense tacit knowledge. The fundamental skills required for *wanch'o* crafts, including hands with a sensitive touch and an acute perception of weight and balance, can only be acquired through countless hours of practice. The goal of this project is twofold: to analyze the traditional and contemporary craft processes involved in *wanch'o* production, and, more generally, to critically examine reconstruction as method in the history of science. To do so, I attempt to reconstruct a circular *wanch'o* mat. Through this reconstruction process, I examine the skills and knowledge required for successful *wanch'o* production to further understand the importance of tacit knowledge with regards to cultures of making. Finally, I critically examine the role of reconstruction in the larger history of science and technology in Korea.

Introduction

> *Entirely handmade Kanghwado wanch'o products express the sincere and dedicated craftsmanship of their maker. It would be no exaggeration to say that I have invested my entire life into the making of sedge handicrafts. I cannot express the exhilaration that I experience whenever I create something out of only sedge material.*

Yi Sang-jae

Anyone who has ventured into the world of "Do It Yourself" (DIY) projects is likely familiar with the various forms of instructional pamphlets, guidebooks, and other types of directions. Often, upon first glance, the instructions appear simple and straightforward enough that the project should progress without much trouble. However, once the person finds themselves in the throes of making, they then realize that there are vital steps missing from the instructions, or the writing is so vague that they cannot figure out how to progress from one step to the next. Or perhaps someone is following a cooking recipe, realizes they are missing some of the necessary ingredients, and must now decide what, if anything, to substitute for these missing ingredients.

This scenario is very similar to what artisans experienced throughout the history of science in Korea. Imagining myself in the position of such an artisan, the necessity of reworking, prototyping, modeling, and general tinkering becomes obvious. Attempting to understand the detailed processes of any given product is nearly impossible without the hands-on experience provided by tinkering. In this case, "making" is truly "knowing," and to separate the two would be to deny the importance of experimentation in empirical processes.[1]

The act of reading instructions and using the information provided to produce a final product or develop a skill is so ubiquitous that it is often taken for granted in

---

[1] For works on Korean artisanship, see Kang, Hyeok Hweon. "Cooking Niter, Prototyping Nature: Saltpeter and Artisical Experiment in Seventeenth-Century Korea." *Isis: A Journal of the History of Science Society* 113, no. 1 (March 2022): 1–21, and Lee, Jung. "Invention without Science: 'Korean Edisons' and the Changing of Technology in Colonial Korea." *Technology and Culture* 54, no. 4 (2013): 782–814.

contemporary discussions. While these written instructions tell us how to interact with things and serve as a way of "knowing," "another means of 'knowing; things might be as simple as trial-and-error." [2] Thus, adding to Smith's efforts of understanding the myriad perspectives of "making and knowing," I set out to conduct a rework project in order to gain insight into empirical modes of reproduction.

At the crux of this research project is my own attempt to recreate a circular *wanch'o* mat primarily using an instructional text with some supplemental video aids. This *wanch'o* reconstruction project is part of a larger course titled "Kitchen, Studio, Factory: Making in East Asia," led by Dr. Hyeok Hweon Kang at Washington University in Saint Louis. Throughout the semester, students engaged in their own "rework project," which involved the exploration of craft practices by reconstructing an object based on historical primary resources. Incorporating a rework project into this research allows for exploration into understanding the rework process as part and parcel of scientific experimentation and discovery in Korea. Drawing on knowledge from the Making and Knowing Project founded by Pamela Smith at Columbia University, this *wanch'o* rework project aims to challenge our contemporary understanding of knowledge production by analyzing the historical intersections of craft and science in Korea. I argue that early Korean artisans took advantage of the existing craft cultures of reconstruction, prototyping, reverse engineering, and modeling. Through these traditional modes of experimentation, these artisan-scientists developed skills that later contributed to what we recognize as the Korean Modern.

Empirical Reconstruction

According to Pamela Smith, the founder of the Making and Knowing Project at Columbia University, the Project is "a new approach to exploring historical texts, one which emphasizes the importance of the material conditions, interpretations, and outcomes that emerge when the written word is realized through investigations into matter." [3] When approaching manuscripts which codify procedures for various types of craft or technological knowledge, it is important to

---

[2] Smith, Pamela H. "In the Workshop of History: Making, Writing, and Meaning." *West 86th: A Journal of Decorative Arts, Design History, and Material Culture* 19, no. 1 (2012): 4–31.

[3] Smith, Pamela H. "About – Making and Knowing Project." https://www.makingandknowing.org/about-the-project/.

consider how these written instructions may translate to embodied skills. Upon even a cursory attempt to recreate a skill or object using an instructional manuscript, it becomes clear that the act of simply reading such manuscripts must be accompanied by the physical act of making. What's more, Jacob Eyferth points out that "writing in itself cannot encode an entire technique in such a way that it may be decoded by people who have no previous knowledge of it."[4]

The nature of the text used for this rework project seems far more informational than instructional. That is, the text describes, step-by-step, how to make a *wanch'o* circular mat, yet it does not provide the details necessary for people unfamiliar with the process to figure it out. I argue that this text was not intended to serve as a "do-it-yourself" guide for people wanting to learn the *wanch'o* craft, but instead is an informational piece for readers more generally interested in the craft and its process, but not actually in making. As Smith points out, these instructional manuscripts are not actually meant to provide full and detailed instructions, but instead provide enough guidance to "an invitation to imitate and experiment."[5]

When examining historical objects today, it is often difficult to fully know the object without an understanding of the creation process for said object. Thus, through various types of rework projects, "an appreciation of the meaning, function, and operation of a historical object can also be gained by a knowledge of how it was made."[6] Thus, we see how empirical reconstruction can serve as a tool for looking towards the future as part of the innovation process, but also for looking at the past, as a way to understand and appreciate the context and meaning of a product.

However, in using reconstruction for looking at either the past or the future, makers are often faced with a myriad of challenges. One of such challenges is the use of manuscripts for reconstruction. "Knowledge of making processes can often be difficult to obtain because it often cannot be conveyed effectively in written description, but rather must be learned on-site by careful and conscious observation."[7] As demonstrated with the *wanch'o* rework project, technical writings seldom provide sufficient instruction and information necessary to actually engage in the process of making. But even when one has the opportunity to observe the

---

[4] Eyferth, Jacob. "Craft Knowledge at the Interface of Written and Oral Cultures." *East Asian Science, Technology and Society: An International Journal* 4, no. 2 (2010): 185–205.

[5] Smith, "About – Making and Knowing Project."

[6] Smith, "In the Workshop of History: Making, Writing, and Meaning."

[7] *IBID.*

making process in real time, the observer cannot always replicate the knowledge gained. It takes time to develop the skills and tacit knowledge that well-practiced artisans often possess. What's more, the development of these skills relies not on instruction, but understanding. That is, through the process of making, one comes to understand the materials and the process on a level far more complex than receiving instruction, whether said instructions are from a written text or from a skilled craftsman.

Global and Domestic Knowledge Production via Reconstruction

By considering reconstruction as an integral part of larger empirical processes, we can also assess its role as a form of knowledge exchange throughout history. Because the development of science and technology in Korea largely involved global knowledge exchange, it is important to consider both a holistic East Asian approach in addition to a specifically Korean approach. Thus, the analysis of Korean knowledge production must adopt a global eye while still acknowledging the aspects of Korean history that are firmly grounded in the domestic sphere.

In her analysis of models as both a material thing and an analytical category in Tokugawa Japan, Christine Guth questions what it means to be a model rather than a copy, and the significance of modeling as a means of innovation. From the western perspective, the acts of modeling and copying are often conflated and given a negative connotation. These acts are seen as imitation, yet, as Guth points out, "'copy of' and 'model for' – the former may have negative connotations of temporal and developmental backwardness while the latter projects a more proactive image."[8] The extensive amount of English language literature focusing on the copy tends to damage the concept of the model as an integral part of the innovation process. What's more, this literature often associates modeling practices with the East, while privileging the West with a reputation as original innovators.

Yet, the culture of modeling and reconstruction has remained a persistent part of East Asian innovation. Countries such as China, Japan, and Korea have demonstrated exceptional success with adapting scientific and industrial technology through various stages of reconstruction.

---

[8] Guth, Christine. "Modeling, Models, and Knowledge Exchange in Early Modern Japan." *RES: Anthropology and Aesthetics* 71–72 (2019): 253–64.

Wanch'o Rework Project

What is Wanch'o?

According to the Chronicles of the Three Kingdoms *(Samguksagi)*, *wanch'o*, a type of sedge weaving craft, was being used as early as the Silla period (57 BCE – 935 CE). the mats were used as early as the Silla period and during the Koryŏ period, Korean kings regularly participated in various rituals and sacrificial rites during which *wanch'o* mats were placed under the mortuary tables to help summon the deities. The Ch'osŏn Dynasty Shirhak *(Ch'osŏnwangjosirhak)* describes *wanch'o* products as a valuable possession for members of the royal family and the elite class. Additionally, *wanch'o* products were regularly included as tribute items presented during envoy missions to China.

However, it should also be noted that *wanch'o* products had a decidedly domestic reputation and could be easily recognized as a symbol of Korean domestic spaces. Art Historian Christine Hahn briefly discusses North Korea's use of *wanch'o* mats in an art exhibition from the 1950s. This art exhibit used everyday objects juxtaposed against each other or placed against a decorative screen in order to orient the objects within a recognizably traditional Korean domestic space. Hahn argues that the *wanch'o* mats serve two functions: as objects in their own right as well as the contextual signal for a traditional Korean domestic space.[9] Thus, it is evident that *wanch'o* products have long been valued for both their practicality and their aesthetic properties.

Sedge is a rush-like plant that can be commonly found in wet ground. In Korea, the waterlogged soil of rice paddies is perfect for sedge cultivation and sedge can be found in nearly every village throughout the peninsula. *Wanch'o* products were practical, everyday items that could be made from readily available materials and these items were prized possessions through all social classes. Every stage of *wanch'o* is completed by hand, though there are a few tools involved. *Wanch'o* products included mats, boxes, seat cushions, and even clothing items such as hats, shoes, and bags. Yi Sang-jae, a notable figure in contemporary *wanch'o* studies, is currently the only master sedge weaver *(wanch'ojang)* in South Korea and is the designated bearer of *wanch'o* as an Important National Intangible Cultural Heritage Item. Yi comes from a family of weavers and was considered a *wanch'o*

---

[9] Hahn, Christine Y. "Crafting Koreanness: How Korean National Identity Became Interwoven with the Handmade Object in the Twentieth Century." In *Exhibiting Craft and Design*, 1st ed., 39–55. Routledge, 2017.

expert from an early age. Although *wanch'o* products did enjoy long-standing and widespread popularity, they were eventually replaced by mass-produced products that could serve the same purpose at a lower price. However, Yi doubts that any machine could match the intricate craftsmanship that goes into the making of *wanch'o* products.[10]

Every step of the *wanch'o* production process requires tacit knowledge of understanding how tightly to weave, the material properties of sedge and how it acts when woven in different ways, and how to properly execute the *wanch'o* weaving technique. Tacit knowledge relies on one's senses and intimacy with the materials and products related to the craft. Furthermore, Eyferth describes tacit knowledge as "experiential and embodied knowledge."[11] According to Yi Sang-jae, "The most important aspect of sedge craftsmanship is ensuring that the woven strands have been properly created and evenly rendered...As a successful outcome rests solely on the touch of your hands, a significant amount of concentration is required from start to finish."[12] The fundamental skills required for *wanch'o* crafts, including hands with a sensitive touch and an acute perception of weight and balance, can only be required through countless hours of practice. These days, *wanch'o* is seen as a dying art form, as there are very few people continuing the practice.

Resources Consulted for Rework Project

The primary instructional source consulted for this project was a book titled *Wanch'ojang* (translated in English as *Master Sedge Weaver*) which was published by the National Research Institute of Cultural Heritage in 1999. This is a Korean language text with no English translation and is a comprehensive review of *wanch'o*, including its history, sedge cultivation processes, crafting tools, manufacturing processes, weaving patterns, and current practitioners. All English translations of this text are my own. For the full set of instructions, as well as my translations, see Appendix 1. Although this text is not necessarily historical, it was published as an official guide to *wanch'o* as an Important National Intangible Cultural Heritage Item and is the most detailed textual explanation for the *wanch'o* production process. However, it should be noted that despite the detailed explanation of

---

[10] Lee, Hye-min. "Lee Sang-Jae: The Weft and Warp of Traditional Sedge, Rush Weaving." Korean Culture and Information Service. July, 2018.

[11] Eyferth, "Craft Knowledge at the Interface of Written and Oral Cultures."

[12] *IBID.*

wanch'o production processes, this book does not provide sufficient information. If we consider the title, *Wanchojang (Master Sedge Weaver)*, et becomes evident that this book is focused on the practitioner (Yi) more than the practice.

In addition to this official text, I have consulted several videos of Master Weaver Yi Sang-Jae producing *wanch'o* products and discussing his own production process. Because this weaving process requires a skilled hand and technique developed over a long period of time, I relied on videos to supplement my instruction in ways that the text alone could not. Watching Yi go through the process is closer to the original master-artisan relationship than simply reading a textual description of the text accompanied by a few photographs.

Considering that Yi Sang-Jae came from a lineage of *wanch'o* artisans, it is likely that he learned this craft through some type of master-apprentice relationship. No matter how detailed the written instructions may be, this type of craft necessitates a live instructor. Guth describes the importance of a master-apprentice relationship as "communication using bodily demonstration, rather than propositional communication reliant on words." [13] Of course, with modern technology we now have access to videos and tutorials to learn new skills. Although I was unable locate any detailed tutorials of how to make *wanch'o* crafts, being able to see the process in action helped me understand what the written instructions meant. Without the video aids, this project would have required much more trial and error and experimentation, a process I expect many historical craftspeople in Korea would have been familiar with.

Considering the Materiality of Wanch'o

Wanch'o is known to have come from Kyodongdo Island in Kanghwa-kun County, which has unfavorable soil conditions for rice farming. Thus, sedge and reed plants are a key agricultural product for the community. With such an abundance of sedge available, sedge weaving became a popular craft in this part of the country. Historically, many members of this community make a living selling *wanch'o* products, such as artisan Yi and his family.

The process starts with the sedge planting and harvesting which begins in April and lasts until August. The sedge stalks are cut into strands and dried for several months. Once the strands turn a bluish color, they are soaked in water then dried in the sun. The soak/dry process is then repeated five to six times until the sedge

---

[13] Guth, "Modeling, Models, and Knowledge Exchange in Early Modern Japan."

strands turn white. For colored strands, there is an additional hand-dyeing process. Once the materials have been prepared, different weaving patterns can be implemented to create different products.

Although unable to access to any pre-processed sedge with which to weave, I obtained a variety of materials to work with and find out what best imitates sedge. Because sedge is a grass, another weaving fiber such as rush or reed seemed to make a good replacement. However, it quickly became apparent that neither reed, nor rush, would be a good option, since both these materials are not flexible enough for the tightly woven *wanch'o* process. Thus, I purchased three potential options: rolled paper, cotton yarn, and a waxed cotton cord (Figure 1).

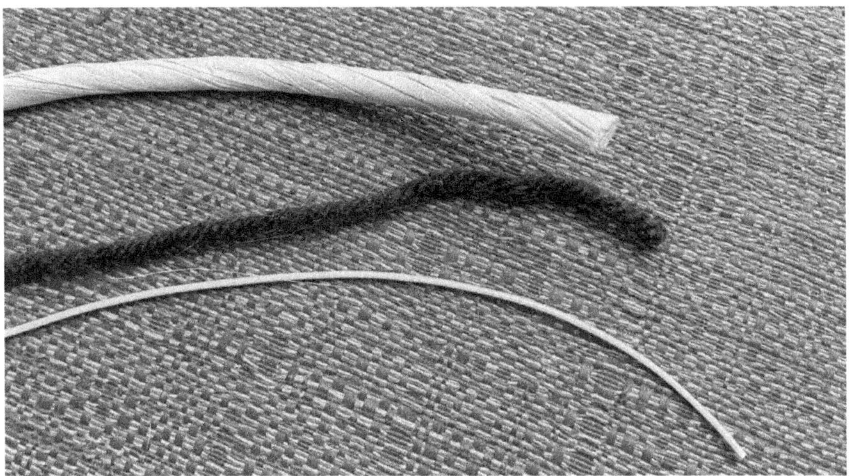

Figure 1: From top to bottom: rolled paper, cotton yarn, and waxed cotton cord

The rolled paper had a similar flexibility/stiffness to sedge but the actual strands were too thick, thus unable to be easily and tightly woven. The yarn, however, was far too flexible, fibrous, and difficult to handle. Because this weaving process happens without a loom, the strands need to have a certain degree of rigidity, while still being flexible enough to be tightly woven. The waxed cotton cord was the best option because of its slick texture, size, and slight rigidity. Ideally, the cord would have been more flat than round in order to better imitate the materiality of the sedge, but I was unable to locate such cord.

Rework Project Process and Reflections

Neither the text nor the videos consulted provide concrete instructions for how to begin the weaving process. Although the text briefly describes the steps to get started, it only tells the reader *what* to do but not *how* to do it. Once I started to weave the warp and the weft together, I realized that the instructional materials only enabled me to visualize this process, but not properly make a *wanch'o* product without proper prior training.

As demonstrated in the photographs, the center of the circular mat is overcrowded with the warp strands because I started with the incorrect number of strands. However, as the circle's diameter began to increase, it became apparent that the *wanch'o* product resembled the other circular mats I've seen. According to the next instruction, the warp threads increase as the diameter of the circle increases and the weaver adds warp strands every couple of rounds, doubling the number of warp strands in the circle. The videos provided no information about how to add warp strands, and the shots showing Yi adding strands are from angles that don't allow for a full visualization of the process.

I misinterpreted the process of doubling the strands as adding a single blade that has been folded in half, thus resulting in two strands being added to the circle each time. If my *wanch'o* product is closely inspected, the loops where the strands have been doubled over are somewhat visible. After a series of trial-and-error attempts, I now believe that the strands are added one at a time between existing strands, thus doubling the number of strands that existed before the new ones were added.

An additional issue that emerged was controlling the tension in my hands while weaving. As a beginner, I did not have the tacit knowledge necessary to know whether or not my weaving was too tight or too loose. As I progressed with my circle, I realized that the center was beginning to take on a dome shape rather than lay flat (Figure 2). I was able to solve this problem by adjusting my tension to be more consistent, and by laying the mat out on a flat surface while I wove instead of holding it in my hands and letting it naturally fall into a dome shape.

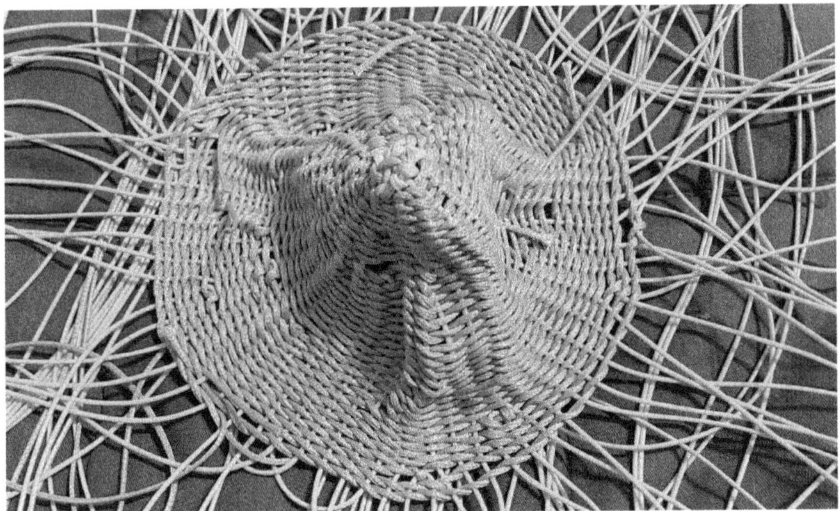

Figure 2: The "finished" *wanch'o* product with dome-shaped center

Despite nearly every text and video about *wanch'o* emphasizing the skill and patience required for the craft, I severely underestimated the amount of time the weaving would take. As an experienced knitter, crocheter, and cross-stitcher, I thought my skills would transfer well for *wanch'o*. And while some of the skills did transfer, such as steady hands and excellent fine motor skills, *wanch'o* is an entirely different craft which cannot be learned in a single sitting. Over the course of four days, I wove for a total of approximately fifteen hours and was still unable to complete the product. However, the double-edge weaving pattern characteristic of *wanch'o* crafts was rather simple to follow and resembled that of professionally crafted *wanch'o* products (Figure 3).

Although I made several mistakes that affected the appearance of my final product, through the process of reconstruction I was able to test different methods based on a combination of visual aids and my own tacit knowledge. Prior to starting the project, I thought I would have a relatively easy time figuring it out because the text is quite detailed when compared to many other East Asian historical craft texts. In my head I could go through all the steps. It was only once I had the strands in my hand that I realized I had little idea how to put these steps into practice.

Figure 3: Close up image of interwoven warp and weft using the *wanch'o* weaving technique

Understanding Reconstruction and Empiricism

An engagement with and analysis of *Wanch'ojang* as an instructional manuscript reveals that reconstruction exists at the intersection of craft and science. The reconstruction process can range from a casual curiosity, to an analytical and intensely rigorous project. In either case, the result is a more nuanced understanding of the various components that come together to make a product. The most significant hurdle encountered during the *wanch'o* rework project was the lack of a teacher to develop the skills and tacit knowledge required for *wanch'o* craft work. That is, without the master-apprentice relationship, the reliance on a written manuscript creates space for greater interpretation of the text.

To further elaborate the significance of tact knowledge, Smith notes that "skill grows out of human interaction with the natural environment, and out of this attentive and collective experience come all the remarkable products of human culture."[14] Thus, it could be argued, the development of tacit knowledge is crucial for the process of making and knowing. If we consider tacit knowledge as a result of one's natural environment, then we must grapple with the notion of how to teach a skill. Smith elaborates on the development of skill:

> *There is no textual shortcut to skill. Like learning to play a musical instrument, skill must be acquired alongside an experienced practitioner, performed methodically by means of observing, attending,*

---

[14] Smith, "In the Workshop of History: Making, Writing, and Meaning."

and repeating through years of experience until the coordination of perception and action becomes habit. Learning is primarily about not the transmission of information, but the education of the attention. And skill cannot be learned except by "doing," involving many years (ten thousand hours, according to cognitive psychologists) of practice, usually under the watchful eye of an expert practitioner.[15]

With this approach, the student is able to witness the teacher not only teach via verbal instruction, but also teach through action and demonstration. The student then reconstructs the actions of the teacher, repeating the cycle until the student masters whatever skill is being taught.

Although the possibility of interpretation of the *Wanch'ojang* manuscript resulted in a final product different from the initial target for this project, it also allows for an opportunity to discover new or alternatives modes of engagement with the materials used throughout the process. Despite written manuscripts having long served as the optimal mode for the preservation and spread of technical knowledge, it is the space "between the lines" that enables artisans, and later scientists, to further adapt and innovate.

Furthermore, reconstruction offers insight into the ways in which artisans and consumers may have interacted with a product. Understanding the processes involved with production, a product's value (social, monetary, aesthetic, etc.), is especially important for historians. When any given product is removed from its socio-temporal context, historians can engage in reconstruction processes as a means of further gaining knowledge about the object, its materiality, its purpose, and more.

Empirical Reconstruction, Adaptation, and Innovation in the Korean Historical Context

Postcolonial South Korea

When looking at more contemporary examples of reconstruction for the sake of innovation in Korea, the case of the power tiller and the Apple II computer should be discussed. The process of modernization and mechanization in postcolonial South Korea is well known for having occurred over such a relatively short period

---

[15] *IBID.*

of time. As a result, there was a number of economic plans instituted by the government and an increase in commercialization and corporate presence. Hyungsub Choi offers up the story of the power tiller, "not simply as an episode in the universal spread of the American ideal of agricultural mechanization, but as a highly local phenomenon contingent upon political, social and economic conditions of the nation undergoing rapid development."[16] The combination of an imported foreign technology along with a rapidly changing industrial environment meant that there were several "gaps" in the power tiller use and technology. These gaps should be understood as areas where the technology and/or its use can be further altered or improved to better fit a different environment. In an attempt to fill these gaps, developers localized the power tiller technology and adapted its use to fit their own domestic needs.

These power tillers are a unique case for studying reconstruction as a tool for innovation. Rather than relying on a manuscript for understanding the inner workings of this technology, technicians had to deal with the issue of adapting the foreign power tiller to their own domestic environment. For this process, technicians first replicated the imported Japanese power tillers, then made subtle adjustments to better fit their local context. Choi points out that "the Korean power tillers could hardly be called 'innovation' or the 'creation of the new,' [but] South Korean businessmen and policymakers still prided themselves on achieving a near-complete localization of foreign technology.[17] The act of reverse engineering these foreign products gave these technicians the opportunity to identify their own domestic needs and reconfigure the power tiller technology accordingly.

In the case of the Apple II computer, Jo discusses the "vernacular technical practices" that developed in relation to the computer industry. These vernacular practices are those that developed in relation to the larger population and are not exclusive to the social and political elite. Jo argues that the vernacular technical practice of cloning, though not considered an "official" practice, actually constitutes "a critical part of the computer industry and the history of

---

[16] Choi, Hyungsub. "Imported Machines in the Garden: The Kyongun'gi (Power Tiller) and Agricultural Mechanization in South Korea." *History and Technology: An International Journal* 33, no. 4 (2017): 345–66.

[17] *IBID.*

computing."[18] As was the case with many different technologies, not just the Apple II computer, technicians working within these vernacular technical practices were often on the cutting edge of technological innovation, sometimes before their counterparts in the West. These technicians tinkered with the technologies, rethinking their potential uses and adaptations which, in turn, resulted in new and innovative ideas and technologies.

Jo notes that, in the Korean context, clones were often seen as better than the original in almost every aspect because, "the local practitioners of cloning acquired not only knowledge of the original technical artifacts through the process of reverse-engineering and reproducing them, but they were also familiar with the specific situations in which they would actually be used."[19] Similarly, Choi reveals that "it was only through relaxing the expected role to be played by power tillers in agricultural practice that policymakers and farmers could justify their wider dissemination."[20] While the computer cloning was primarily happening in spaces where the vernacular technical practices were in tune with the local needs, the power tillers seemed to face a reversed situation. The government policies surrounding agriculture, land ownership, and general usage of the power tillers made it more difficult for power tillers to gain traction as a valuable item for household farmers. Instead, the government slowly responded to the reactions of farmers and widened the acceptable usage of power tillers.

The cases of power tillers and Apple II computers aptly demonstrate the value of imitation and adaptation. Choi and Jo both parse out the historical realities of Korean industrialization during a compressed modernization. By looking at imitation and cloning, combined with localized use of the circulating products, Choi and Jo reveal the nuances of adapting technology to specific audiences by using empirical reconstruction. I would argue that imitation is a critical aspect of innovation in that the value of imitation is not the ability to produce an exact copy, but the ability to localize a product or information to a specific context. Technology transfer is not as simple as copy/paste, but instead requires a great deal of understanding how the technology is made, how it can be improved, and how it can be adapted. What's more, identifying these gaps during the technology

---

[18] Jo, Dongwon. "Vernacular Practices Beyond the Imitative/Innovative Boundary: Apple II Cloning In Early-1980s South Korea." *East Asian Science, Technology and Society: An International Journal,* 2021, 1–24.

[19] *IBID.*

[20] Choi, "Imported Machines in the Garden: The Kyongun'gi (Power Tiller) and Agricultural Mechanization in South Korea."

transfer process enables practitioners to find creative solutions and further develop the technology. These skills of imitation are, in fact, quite valuable for understanding the culture of technology production in Korea.

Science and Technology in Contemporary South Korea

As many scholars point out, much of South Korea's recent economic growth is due to the nation's late industrialization policy. Scholars Dong-Won Kim and Stuart Leslie describe South Korea's late industrialization policies as a system that relies on learning rather than initial invention or innovation. South Korea modeled its own late industrialization policies after Japan, which looked to Western nations such as the United States and Germany and thus actively appropriated the West, which is the exact accusation that many western countries seem to make in their own arguments against East Asian "copy culture."[21] Kim and Leslie argue that, as a result of South Korea's late industrialization policy and government initiated industrialization plans, the nation is no longer looking to the West for technological inspiration, but "has embarked on efforts to thrive on its own resources," meaning they are now actively participating in the competitive markets of STEM, including the high-tech industry.[22] This demonstrates that within the contemporary period, the legacy of reconstruction remains strong and its contributions to South Korea's development as an economic powerhouse run deep. While South Korea's late industrialization policies were modeled off of other nations, its success relied on the nation's ability to adapt these policies to their domestic issues. That is not to say that the development of South Korea is without its flaws, but that is a topic for a different paper.

Researcher Sang-Hyun Kim traces the history of science and technology in South Korea in order to understand how the nation's current and prevailing conceptions of the meanings, purposes, and roles of science and technology have been embedded into South Korea's distinctive ideas of nationhood and development. This is part of Kim's larger effort to deconstruct how South Korea's view of science and technology has served as a crucial element of the nation's development that defines "advanced/developed" and "backward/undeveloped," primarily in terms of industrialization and economic growth. Kim uses modernization discourse in order to contextualize the technological development happening in

---

[21] Dong-Won Kim and Leslie W. Stuart, "Winning Markets or Winning Nobel Prizes? Kaist and the Challenges of Late Industrialization," *Osiris* 13 (1998): 154–85.

[22] *IBID.*

South Korea over a short period of time. In terms of understanding the rise of technology in South Korea in conjunction with the rise of globalization, "South Korea has conceived science and technology, first and foremost, as a form of power and as instruments to serve national development, which is defined primarily in terms of autonomous and self-reliant industrialization and economic growth as is presumed as the main goal and obligation of the nation."[23] Kim uses technology as the metric for development in South Korea and historically situates said development through the lens of nationalism. Thus, it can also be argued that innovation itself could and should be studied in relation to Korean nationalism.

From this perspective, reconstruction could also be considered a result of Korean nationalism, yet I am inclined to disagree with this argument. Empirical reconstruction can certainly occur with nationalist motivations, but to only associate the practice with a nationalistic cause severely limits the use and scope of reconstruction as a tool for innovation. Perhaps it would be more fitting to describe empirical reconstruction as a form of nationalism. Doing so does not dismiss the nationalist associational of reconstruction, but still does not place boundaries on our understanding of reconstruction as a tool for experimentation, regardless of the motivation.

Conclusion

Considering reconstruction as an aspect of empirical experimentation can easily be taken for granted, but the history of science and technology in Korea cannot be separated from the practice of reconstruction and its many forms. Such forms include trial-and-error reconstruction based on a written text, reverse engineering of a product, modeling from an existing object, prototyping, and more.

For historians of science, reproducing historical experiments and reworking historical practices offers the unique perspective of the practitioner. Though the concept of experimental reconstruction and rework projects is not new, it has only been adopted by historians in recent years as a means to gain insight into the development of scientific practices. As Fors et al note, "the fundamental aim of all experimental activity is to expand the boundaries of what the experimenter knows, and thus when the historian turns to experiment, his or her primary aim is to use experiments to obtain historical information that cannot be accessed by other

---

[23] Sang-Hyun Kim, "Science, Technology, and the Imaginaries of Development in South Korea," *Development and Society* 46, no. 2 (September 2017): 341–71.

means or from other sources."[24] Historians can use reconstruction as a key to unlocking the knowledge otherwise inaccessible in the existing body of documentary knowledge.

Shifting away from looking to the past, reconstruction can also be employed as a tool for future innovation. As artisans participated in reconstruction, they actively experimented with the materiality of a product and the skills used to produce it, this finding new and adaptive ways to apply a skill or technology to an environment different than what it was originally developed for. In so doing, these artisans innovated where they found gaps in the technologies. These gaps were often due to the importation of foreign knowledge and the necessity of adapting such knowledge to a domestic space. Sometimes these innovations were intentional, such as the adaptations made to the Apple II computers, and sometimes they were accidental, where artisans relied on trial-and-error when dealing with written instructions, drawings, or a single object. However, both intentional and accidental innovation rely on the tacit knowledge of the artisan.

The *wanch'o* rework project demonstrates that the practice of reconstruction as an empirical tool allows for a more nuanced way of knowing. Through reconstruction, the artisan develops not only skill and tacit knowledge, but also an intimate knowledge of materials and how they work together and react differently in different environments and circumstances. For example, because I was unable to use actual processed sedge and instead used waxed cotton cord for weaving, I was able to appreciate the materiality of sedge and its use.

Although this project used *wanch'o* as a case study in the larger argument of reconstruction as part of innovation, further study should be done regarding different types of craft and technology and its legacy. What's more, the possibility of tracing the development of modern technologies and analyzing the different modes of reconstruction used for their development would further expand on our contemporary understanding of reconstruction in the Korean context. Finally, the process of reconstruction and its many forms is not unique to Korea, or any single geographic area. However, reconstruction and its use has developed differently within different cultural context and should thus be studied accordingly. This paper has analyzed the Korean case, but does it differ for other East Asian

---

[24] Fors, Hjalmar, Lawrence M. Principe, and H. Otto Sibum. "From the Library to the Laboratory and Back Again: Experiment as a Tool for Historians of Science." *Ambix* 63, no. 2 (April 2, 2016): 85–97.

countries? In the West? Globally? These are all points to consider for further research.

Appendix

Appendix 1. Instructions from *Wanch'ojang* (완초장(莞草匠)) and English translations provided by author.

1. 가늘게 다듬은 완초 4 날을 반접어 정자형으로 엮어 날줄을 만든다. 그러면 총 8 개 의 날줄이 생긴다. 이 날줄을 두겹씩, 즉 4 날(두날엮기)로 하여 두 개의 씨줄로 엮 는다. 그래서 최초의 날수를 8 개로 하여 시작한다.

   a. Four thinly cut blades of sedge are folded in half and woven into a "T" shape. Then there are a total of eight strands. These strands are woven into two layers using the four blades (double-edged weaving). So we start with the first of the eight strands.

2. 날줄을 추가하면서 원의 지름을 넓혀가는데 날줄은 최초 8 날에서 16, 32, 64, 128, 256 날까지 증가하게 된다. 날줄 수의 증가는 항상 배수로 나아가는데 방석의 크기 가 커질수록 날줄의 수는 이보다 더 증가하게 된다.

   a. As blades are added, the diameter of the circle is widened, and the blades increase from the first eight blades to 16, 32, 64, 128, and 256. The increase in the number of blades is always double, and as the size of the mat increases, the number of blades increases.

3. 정확한 수치는 아니지만 128 의 날줄이 256 개의 날줄로 증가하기 전에 분홍색의 완 초로 장식을 한다. 그리고 분홍색에 다른색(하늘색)을 추가하면서 날줄을 하나씩 추 가하는데, 이때에 256 개의 날줄이 되어 간격이 좁아지게 되면서 색감이 촘촘히 박 히게 된다.

a. Although not an exact number, the 128 blade is decorated with pink strands before increasing to 256 blades. To add a different color (sky blue) to pink, add a blade one by one, and the 256 strands become narrow and the color is densely embedded.

4. 방석의 직경 크기가 어느 정도 되면 씨줄을 하나 더 잡아 3 개의 씨줄로 돌려주는 데, 이것은 "삼오리친다"는 용어로 표현되는 과정이다. 완초공예품 제작과정중에 반 드시 포함되는 중요한 과정이다. 씨줄을 3 개를 넣는 부분(삼오리를 치는 부분)은 소 품의 제작공정상 꺾이거나 접히는 부분에 해당된다. 그래서 꺾이는 부분을 표시하 고 꺾이는 부분이 튼튼하도록 씨줄을 추가하여서 돌려주는 것이다. 4 개의 씨줄로 돌리는(사오리치기)과정이 동그리 제작과정에 나오지만 이것은 소품의 외형을 장식 하기 위한 것이다. 그래서 보통 꺾이거나 접히는 부분은 삼오리치기가 대부분이다.

a. When the diameter of the mat reaches a certain size, one more weft strand is picked up and returned to the three weft strands, which is a process expressed in the term *"samori-chigi."* It is an important process that must be included in the production process of *wanch'o* crafts. The part where three weft strands are put (the part where the three weft strands are hit) corresponds to the part of the product that is bent or folded during the creation process. Therefore, the bent part is marked, and the weft strand is added and returned so that the bent part is strong. The four weft strand weaving process (*saori-chigi*) takes place in the circular production process, but this is to decorate the appearance of the products. So, most of the parts that are usually bent or folded are three strand weaving.

5. 삼오리를 돌린 후 2 개의 씨줄로 1 개의 날줄을 엮어나가는데 1 번을 돌려준후 손으로 삼오리 친 부분을 꺾어주고 방망이로 쳐서 꺾인 부분을 굳혀준다.

    a.   After turning the three strand weave, weave one weft blade with two warp strands, and after returning to the first one, bend the three strand weave with your hand and harden the bent part with a mallet.

6. 방석의 뒷면은 삼오리친 부분을 기준으로 반대로 씨줄과 날줄을 돌려나가는데 삼오 리를 친 후 2 번을 돌릴 때까지는 간격을 곱게 하기 위해 날줄 1 개를 2 개의 씨줄로 돌려나가다가 세 번째 돌릴 때부터 날줄 2 개를 묶어서 씨줄을 돌려나간다. 방석의 뒷면을 날줄의 수가 앞면과 정반대 감소한다. 날줄의 수가 줄어들어야지 방석의 직 경이 좁아지기 때문이다. 256, 128, 64, 32, 16, 8 날의 순서이다.

    a.   The back of the mat is reversed based on the three strand weave, and after hitting the three strand weave, one of the strands is returned to two to make the gap fine until it is turned twice, and from the third turn, two of the ropes are tied to turn the strand. The number of blades on the back of the mat decreases opposite to the front. This is because the diameter of the mat narrows only when the number of blades decreases. The order is 256, 128, 64, 32, 16, and 8.

7. 날줄 8 개를 남기면서 공간을 완전히 메워버리고 이 8 개의 날줄 밑부분을 자른 후에 꼬챙이로 남은 부분을 밀어넣는다. 뒷면의 공간이 뜬부분이나 부풀어 오른 완초를 밀착시키기 위해 방망이로 쳐주며, 방석의 앞면은 방망이의 머리부분으로 밀어주면 서 왕골의 간격과 뜬 공간을 밀착시켜준다. 모든 과정이 끝이 난 것이다.

    a.   Fill up the space by leaving eight of the strands, then cut the ends of the eight strands and push the remaining parts in with a dowel. Hit the space on the back with a mallet in order to flatten the puffy *wanch'o*. The front of the mat is pushed to the head of the mallet to closely adhere the gap between *wanch'o* and the puffy space. The whole process is over

Setting the Tiles of the Print Industry: Reconstructing the *Jikji* and Exploring Korean Empiricism

Sheilly A. Moreno

Abstract

Eighty years before the printing revolution recognized by Gutenberg's Bible in Europe, individuals in East Asia were already well underway with the development of the metal moveable type. While Gutenberg and the West held the title for this new lucrative printing method for a moment in time, in 1972, it was discovered that Korea had actually realized metal type typography a couple of decades before with the Jikji (short for *Paegun-hwasang-ch'orok-pulcho-jikji simch'e-yojŏl*). This paper utilizes reconstruction methodology to dig deeper into the creators of the first noted metal typeface and their thinking to re-contextualize the importance of literacy and early printing culture through an understanding of the constraints and adaptation of Buddhist monks during the Koryŏ period. The tangibility of knowledge through the written word was an impressive feat for humankind, however the ability to transfer several words at a time without room for mistakes, as commonly found through scribe's handwritten copying, revolutionized the print world. I argue that an investigation into reconstruction not only forces one to negotiate shortcomings in written instructions with the tacit knowledge of troubleshooting, but also allows one to acknowledge how each human brain attempts different strategies to reach a solution based on previous experience, whether contextual or non-contextual

Introduction

Reconstruction method is a relatively new academic field of study. It tackles a novel way of analyzing the materiality of items through an exploration of functionality and its relation to their contemporary environments. Pamela Smith, professor at Columbia University and founder of the "Making and Knowing Project" states, "much can be gained by renewing a dialogue among the arts, history, and natural science, and by resuscitating the concept that the investigation of nature and of the human world are deeply entwined."[1] When exploring items from distant periods, many questions arise but only a handful, if any, ever get answered. This is due to the limited amount of written information on several objects we consider today "artifacts". What has transcended and lasted throughout the years as proof that individuals held specific pools of knowledge are merely these tangible items that we now yearn to investigate and create stories for.

In my attribution to this field of study, I will orient my methodology around the idea that experience is worth more than any other source to induce the procurement of knowledge. It is through the active practice of a skill that information is best transmitted since it allows for the interaction of the body with material and thus engages the mind and reinforces tacit knowledge. Smith specifies "there is no textual shortcut to skill."[2] While the limitations of my project are explicit due to the absence of a background in lost-wax casting and metalwork, the transferable skills I have from other material and through engagement with written work can be amplified through the experience I gain from the trial itself. It is crucial to note that many projects within this field currently center around the early craftspeople of Europe and follow the guises of technical writing to piece together the "in-between" of these small documents and their resulting end products. My paper will bring into conversation the artisan knowledge of craft from the perspective of the Korean peninsula, a location often overshadowed by its neighbors in terms of empirical thinking and processes. I bring into the world of reconstruction, a modern take on reconstructing the oldest moveable metal type printed book in order to give way to Korean artisans in the conversation of craftsmanship.

---

[1] Pamela H. Smith "Historians in the Laboratory: Reconstruction of Renaissance Art and Technology in the Making and Knowing Project," (Art History 39.2, 2016): 229.

[2] Pamela H. Smith "In the Workshop of History: Making, Writing, and Meaning." (*West 86th* 19, no. 1, 2012): 7.

My focus and reworking on the *Jikji* guide us through the journey that metal typeface typography pursued after this initial point. While the creators of the *Jikji* were Buddhist monks, separated by degrees of authority and regulation of the central government, their individual knowledge stemmed from being crafters, as well as men of political and economic influence during the Koryŏ dynasty. It is through that lens that I examine the scope of the Buddhist monk's tacit knowledge in handling molten metal and the creation of such artifacts. In regard to this paper, I seek out the answer to whether Buddhist monks transferred skills from creating typefaces out of different materials or utilized observation and knowledge of metalwork to produce such a craft. The art and skill of being able to work with various materials and transfer the lost-wax technique from sculpture making to a revolutionizing technology for the dissemination of the written word. It is through an unspoken wisdom from craftsmen to the centralized government that kicks off a history of typography in Korea. It is important to take note that the metal typeface created by the monks was not an isolated 'craft' or innovative piece of technology but a chapter in the long history of print production and innovation, thus, pairing it with woodblock printing and wooden moveable type. I argue that an investigation into reconstruction not only forces one to negotiate shortcomings in written instructions with the tacit knowledge of troubleshooting, but also allows one to acknowledge how each human brain attempts different strategies to reach a solution based on previous experience, whether contextual or non-contextual. It is through subjective investigation that hidden truths are revealed about artifacts and extrapolated to fill in the gap of understanding between technical writings and finished pieces.

Jikji and Typography in Korea

Jikji, short for *Paegun-hwasang-ch'orok-pulcho-jikji simch'e-yojŏl* in English *Anthology of Great Buddhist Priests' Zen Teaching*, is a Buddhist book detailing how one can follow in the steps of great Buddhist priests written by a Koryŏ monk named Paekun (백운) that was printed using moveable metal type in 1377 at Hŭngdŏk temple near Chŏngju.[3] The book was originally composed of two volumes, volume one has not been found, but there are 39 pages of volume two in possession. Today, only volume two has been preserved at the National Library in France. While this portion of the *Jikji* is the only evidence of metal moveable type, thanks to woodblock print versions of the *Jikji*, scholars have been able to make out the

---

[3] Seung-cheol Lee, Traces of Jikji and Korean movable metal types in commemoration of the 10th anniversary. (Cheongju City: Cheongju Early Printing Museum, 2013).

missing characters and components. In September of 2001, UNESCO recognized the *Jikji* in the Culture Property List and acknowledged its stance in the world as the first book to ever be printed using metal moveable type. This acknowledgement replaced the 42-line Gutenberg Bible as the oldest printed book in history.[4]

As mentioned previously, the original moveable metal typeface *Jikji* currently resides in the manuscript department at the Nationale Bibliothéque de France. According to the UNESCO recognition document submitted by Korea during 2000, *Jikji* was taken by a French ambassador to Korea named Victor Collin de Plancy from Seoul in 1887 during the reign of King Gojong and was donated to the national library in 1950 where it has remained in the possession of France ever since.[5] It was in 1972 that Dr. Park Byeong-Seon sought out to identify the book's method of composition and due to various studies examining the composition of the ink printing, was able to identify that this was in fact printed with metal type and not wood or clay.

It is important to note the circumstances surrounding the emergence of the moveable metal type in Korea and what exactly led to the innovation of the *Jikji* in the first place. The Koryŏ dynasty (918 CE -1392 CE) of the Korean peninsula encompassed the region that is now South Korea and a portion of North Korea, excluding the eastmost regions. As a Buddhist state, an abundance of culture and literature was produced by the Buddhist individuals of the society.[6] Their achievements throughout this period included and weren't limited to paper, printing, paintings, and sculptures. Aside from the cultural aspects, Buddhist monks were also an integral part of the government and political composition of the state, so much so that the fall of the dynasty is attributed to the corruption and rise of sects of Buddhism that emerged across the centuries.[7]

As a close tribute with Song China (960 CE-1279 CE) next door, Koryŏ was able to engage in a widespread culture of books and other forms of entertainment. Song China was also home to the first wooden moveable type, believed to be established

---

[4] Ki-Jeong Rha, "Memory of the World Register- Nomination Form Republic of Korea- Buljo Jikji simcha yojeol (vol.II)" (UNESCO, MOW Register, 2000).

[5] *IBID*. See more on the discussion to relocate the Jikji back to Korea in Richard Pennington's Jikji, and one NGOS's Lonely Fight to Bring it Home, 2019.

[6] Vermeersch, Sem. The Power of the Buddhas: The Politics of Buddhism during the Koryo Dynasty (918-1392). 1st ed. Vol. 303. Harvard University Asia Center, 2008. https://doi.org/10.2307/j.ctt1x07z5r.

[7] *IBID*.

around this same period. The resources of the Korean peninsula and those of China differed, therefore it is reasonable to see the emergence of a similar technique through two distinct mediums, one utilizing wood and the other metal.[8] The *Jikji* was printed during late Koryŏ, meaning that the Buddhist hold on the dynasty was waning and the dissemination of the Buddha's teachings were a possible last attempt at holding the people's favor. Buddhist monks of the time sought out various ways to either maintain their individual power or to attempt and repair the dissonance between the sects and government. Despite the ultimate fall of the dynasty, moveable metal type went on to find itself a place within Korean society through the subsequent centuries and form a long history of typography.

With the rise of the Chosŏn Dynasty (1392 CE -1910 CE) and the first king, T'aejo, woodblock print was utilized for printing books depicting the previous dynasty. Yet it was not until his grandson T'aejong that the national foundry, *Jujaso*, was established in February of 1403.[9] This national foundry took it upon itself to print hundreds of books to bring into circulation within the Korean society as an absence of books was an issue and importing these items from China was unavailable. The variable typefaces that emerged from Buddhist temples and noncentralized offices around the state were replaced by state standardized typefaces and fonts commissioned directly by the capital of the dynasty. Through the development of the Confucian state, the world of communication and print was able to develop. It reached an all-time high during the reign of Sejong the Great. The first mention of the national foundry is during an entry for Year 3, Month 3, Day 24 that states:

> *The King bestowed 120 bottles of wine on the typecasting foundry. Previously, book-printing involved lining up movable type pieces on a copper plate. Then yellow beeswax was boiled and poured over them, which hardened and set them firmly in place. After that the printing was undertaken. The process consumed a great amount of wax, and not more than a few sheets could be printed in one day. This time, the King personally directed the operation. He ordered Minister of Works Yi Cheon 李蕆 and the former Vice Director 前少尹 Nam*

---

[8] UNESCO "Wooden moveable-type printing of China" accessed April 12, 2022. https://ich.unesco.org/en/USL/wooden-movable-type-printing-of-china-00322

[9] Si-baek Pak, Pak Si-baek ŭi Chosŏn wangjo sillok = The annals of the Joseon dynasty. (2015). V2, V3

Geup 南汲 to reforge the copper plate and standardize the shape of the type pieces. They did not take the time to melt wax, yet the type pieces did not move. The printed text was very precise, and from dozens to as many as 100 pages were printed each day.[10]

The use of beeswax as a sealant for the final printing set up stands out as the characters were not typically standardized and needed additional support to remain in place during the printing process. This process required a piece of paper to be placed on top and the characters transferred through an ink-rubbing technique. This is also the first record within the *Annals of King Sejong* in which the standardization of the typefaces themselves is introduced alongside a unification of the various font types utilized.[11] Of course, this was only the start of the printing industry and book market in Korea, throughout Chosŏn they developed metal moveable type for Han'gul as well and incorporate new methods for casting. Various techniques were sampled such as the creation of wooden models used to create sand molds in which molten bronze was poured over to create the typefaces. These techniques consequently adapted and evolved as time passed and Korea received an influx of information from external sources.[12]

Prior Scholarship

I am not the first scholar to stumble upon the *Jikji* and integrate it into the world of reconstruction. For as long as the *Jikji* has been around, individuals have been seeking the secrets of its construction and innovation. As a contender to the Gutenberg Bible for the world's oldest book printed using metal moveable type, the world desired to learn more. Due to the lack of technical writing focusing on the construction of the metal moveable type, historians relied on other pieces of information to date the *Jikji* as well as use these as primary sources for their own reconstruction. During its debut event in the 1970s, the *Jikji* was examined to source the printing method behind its creation. This examination led to the identification of metal printing in Korea and sparked nationwide interest in placing this item as a piece of intangible culture. The majority of my resources are

---

[10] Si-baek Pak, Pak Si-baek ŭi Chosŏn wangjo sillok = The annals of the Joseon dynasty (2015). V4

[11] For more information on Early Korean typography see Sohn Pow-key (also found as Son Po-gi). Pow-Key Sohn, Early Korean typography (Seoul: Po Chin Chai, 2015).

[12] Hee-Jae Lee, "Korean Typography in 15th century" (World Library and Information Congress: 72nd IFLA General Conference and Council. Seoul, Korea. 2006)

domestic from Korea, as the *Jikji* is not a well-known item outside of the country.[13] These sources do not examine the *Jikji* as a piece for retrieving invaluable material culture but instead focus on identifying the original procedure.

I began this investigation by looking into Park Moon-Year's scholarship on *Jikji* through his article titled, "A Study on the Type Casting, Setting and Printing Method of 'Buljo-Jikji-Simche-Yojeol'" in which the associations regarding Koryŏ and the original procedure of the *Jikji* were examined. Park Moon-Year who has a couple different articles on the *Jikji* and reworking this item as a pivotal moment for human development in the book and print world. One particular study of his besides the summary of *Jikji* and its typeface process took a look at the emerging "movable soil-types", including the history of this technique as utilized in the 18th century, a while away from that of the *Jikji* and metal types.[14] It was through Cho Hyŏng-Jin's restoration process that I could truly understand the *Jikji* through a form of rework methodology. His scholarship not only recreated the individual typefaces from scratch through the "Wax Casting" method, noted within this paper as the lost-wax casting method, but also replicated the oil-soot ink utilized by the Koryŏ dynasty. His particular study goes as far as to identifying the exact components and ratio of items utilized for the clay molds as well as the variation in different Beeswax components.[15]

Other Korean scholars such as Kim Sung-Soo have conducted similar studies in which they attempt to identify the actual method that was utilized to create the metal moveable types utilized in the remaining version of the *Jikji*. During Kim's study, he recreated the metal moveable types out of both a lost wax casting method and a sand-casting methodology.[16] He then compared the two products and realized that unlike the conventional thought of the Koryŏ metal type being made from the lost-wax casting method, it would appear that the sand cast method produced types with a closer finish to the ones utilized in the *Jikji* due to the uneven

---

[13] While digging deeper into why this item is not as explored outside of the nation's boundaries despite residing in a Western country is outside of the scope for my project, it would be interesting to pursue further in another experiment, or even an extension of this essay.

[14] Moon-Year Park, "A Study on the Technique of Printing with Movable Soil-Types in Korea" *Journal of the Institute of Bibliography* issue 39. (2008): 5-29.

[15] Hyŏng-jin Cho, *Chikchi' powŏn yŏn'gu: Koryŏ sidae millap cujopŏp kŭmsŏk hwalcha inswaesul = A study on restoration of Jikji: metal typography of wax casting method of Korye Dynasty* (Han'guk Haksul Chŏngbu, 2009) 6-9.

[16] Kim, Sung-Soo. Paegun hwasang ŭi 'musim' e kwanhan sŏji chŏk yŏn'gu (A Bibliographical Study of the Concept of 'No-Mind' of the Monk Paegun). Han'guk munhŏn chŏngbo hakhoe chi (Journal of the Korean Society for Library and Information Science, 2016) 4: 119–46.

heights produced by the sand-casting method, whereas the beeswax method created more uniform and leveled heights within the typeface. This however is not to discount that the lost-wax casting method was never utilized in the production of metal types in the 13th century, but that it was not the method for this remaining volume. Each of the procedures utilized can be identified throughout the history of Korea and therefore are fair to be assumed as plausible original procedures. Overall, scholarship on the *Jikji* was analyzed through a variety of different means to identify the scope of the materiality surrounding its creation and not the tacit knowledge of the monks and individuals that first encountered metal type casting. In reorienting previous scholarship focusing on the *Jikji* and reworking scholarship with a centralization on dismantling eurocentrism, I hope to embed Korea on the global playing field as a contributor of culture by examining the flexibility of tacit knowledge through a shift in materials while attempting to preserve the procedure and innate human knowledge that goes into craft.

Experimentation

My experimentation procedure was broken into four separate sections based on, master craftsman, Ŏ Guk Chin's lost-wax method rework of *Jikji* during the late 1990s which was translated by Park Moon-Year.[17] As mentioned in the earlier section, speculation has been made as to what method was primarily utilized for the creation of the metal moveable types of the *Jikji,* there is scholarship that attributes later creation of metal moveable types to a sandcast method where characters were carved out of wood and then pressed into trays of sand.. These two methods take months and an array of different masters to complete, below is the detailed procedure for the Beeswax Lost-wax method attributed to creating the metal typeface of the *Jikji* as written by scholar Park Moon-Year following Ŏ Guk Chin's rework.[18]

---

[17] Moon-Year Park, "A Study on the Type Casting, Setting and Printing Method of "Buljo-Jikji-Simche-Yojeol"" Gutenberg-Jahrbuch Koreanischer Buchdruck (1998): 32 – 46.

[18] Park, "A Study on the Type Casting, Setting and Printing Method of "Buljo-Jikji-Simche-Yojeol.""

Making Model Characters:

1. Select model character forms. Character forms can be taken from the printer's own calligraphic writing, a copy of a famous calligrapher's writing, or a printed text.
2. Write down the selected character forms on paper. When a printed copy is used, one may not be able to find all the characters needed. In this case, those missing characters from the reference material are hand-written and supplemented.

Making Prototypes:

1. Based on the shape and size of the selected model character forms, prepare separate or connected trays, and pour molten beeswax or paraffin wax into the trays.
2. When the trays filled with wax cool, stick the model character form paper onto the hardened wax by face down.
3. Cut out the father prototypes spoken as "abija" (아비자). If trays are connected, cut off father prototypes character by character.
4. Trim the abija to refine the shape and thickness of each character.
5. Smooth the surface of each character and trim to make sure they are uniform in size.
6. With beeswax sticks, make branches as necessary and attach abija on the tip of each branch.

Casting:

1. Prepare a casting pot made of wood or metal that can resist high temperature. A branch-shaped beeswax stick with abija is to be placed in the pot.
2. Mix kaolin, clay, or desalinated sand with water to produce the dough to fill the casting pot.
3. Place the casting pot on a level plate. Put the beeswax stick with abija and pour the mixed dough until it fills the pot. Make sure to prevent the occurrence of air bubbles while filling the pot. At this point, make a hole to pour molten iron into the hardened dough, a route for molten iron to run smoothly to the inside, and another hole to let out exhaust gas.
4. When the dough hardens, fire the casting pot so that the beeswax stick with abija completely melts down. Then mother prototypes spoke as "eomija" (어미자) are created inside the dough.

5. Fire the box to a certain degree to help molten iron run smoothly to the inside.

6. Melt metal to be used to cast types

7. Place the box on a level plate and fix the four corners of the box to prevent it from shaking. Pour molten iron through the prepared hole.

8. When molten iron cools down in the casting box, remove the hardened dough and pull out the iron stick with metal types.

9. Cut off created metal types character by character using iron saw.

10. Trim each piece with file and sandpaper.

11. Place the completed metal types in labeled wooden boxes according to a certain order for future use.

Printing Method:

1. Prepare a fixed printing plate that has four fixed edges and each boundary lines on the top and bottom of the page. If possible, prepare two printing plates. While one plate is being used for printing, the other can be prepared for typesetting. Repeating this process saves time.

2. In the center of the printing plate, place embellishments such as Eomi, black barrier bar spoken as "Heukgu" (흑구), title of between folding mark spoken as "Panshimje" (반심제) and pagination spoken as "Jangcha" (장차) that indicate the position of the book folding mark for bookbinding. Pour beeswax into the printing plate until it reaches a point 2-3 mm lower than the boundary lines.

3. When the printing plate is ready, a knowledgeable person reads out the text or book to be printed. This person was called "Changjun" (창준).

4. As Changjun reads, a person called "Moonsungong" (문선경) finds the corresponding character types.

5. When Moonsungong collects all the types that will fill one printing plate, the plate with beeswax is fired so that the surface becomes even. Then, set types into plates.

6. When type setting is finished, fire the printing plate again to smooth out any remaining unevenness of the beeswax.

7. Using a tweezer-like tool spoken as "hwaljadajige" (활자다지게) to adjust and level the typeface. The person responsible for this task was called "Gyunjajang" (견자장).

8. When the types are well set, apply ink to the surface of the types on the printing plate with a brush.

9. Place a piece of paper on the plate and rub it with the "inche" (인체) (horsehair brushes or lumps of wool) to produce the first copy. The person who undertook this task was called "Inchuljang" (인출장).

10. Check the first copy to see if there are any errors or omissions. Mark off the misprinted areas in red and blue ink. When the corrections are done, the "Gyujajeongja" (규자정자) and "Gyujajang: (규자장) pit their signature on the copy. Ultimately it was the "Gamgyogwan" (감교관) who was responsible for correcting the main text.

11. Repair the printing plate according to the corrections made on the first copy and make as many prints as planned or demanded. A person called "Gamingwan" (가민관) was in charge of this.

12. The printed copies are sent to the bindery, where books are bound and kept in storage.

Now due to the scope and limitations of my environment I will be making necessary adjustments to this procedure in order to fit both my resources and skill levels. Below is a detailed list of my limitations and restrictions:

I am not a licensed metalworker, therefore unable to work with molten metal to create typefaces out of bronze or iron.

Instead, I will be using epoxy resin to construct my typeface prototypes.

The original procedure calls for a kaolin clay and sand mixture for the typeface molds, this however takes approximately a month to harden and dry.

Instead, I will be using liquid silicone to create reusable molds for the resin as these take 1-2 days to cure.

While a complete page recreation would have been the goal of this study, due to time and lack of skill, I have reduced the scope to encompass 30 pieces of metal moveable type from two separate pages of the Jikji. 30 characters seemed like an adequate amount to carve and obtain a mental map of the scale and knowledge that went into the craft.

30 characters were carved out of cosmetic level beeswax and 15 of these were utilized to create prototypes.

Hanji and traditional oil soot ink were made from scratch and used during the printing process. However, due to my project centering on the skills of the metal typeface itself, I utilized fine Hanji paper and acrylic black paint due to the texture of the resin and for fear that traditional black ink utilized for calligraphy would not stick onto the resin.

With these adjustments and limitations in mind, the revised procedure below was utilized.

Making Model Characters

1. Utilizing the National Library of France scanned version of the *Jikji*, select one page of reference and download directly from source.
2. Once the image is downloaded, reverse the image by flipping it vertically prior to printing. This will assure that you have a mirrored version to carve the letters out.
3. Cut out strips of reference sheet.

Making Prototypes

1. Obtain Beeswax bars and cut into smaller bars with widths of 1 cm.
2. Attach strips of reference paper to each individual bar of wax.
3. Take a carving tool and cut individual characters abija 아비자 out of the wax.
4. Repeat until all of the characters are cut out.
5. Level characters by trimming smooth backside.

Casting

1. Prepare liquid silicone kit.
2. Set the wax molds in the liquid silicone and allow to cure for 24 hours.
3. After the molds have cured, remove the wax abjia and discard.
4. Inspect the molds for any missing details, correct if missing details.
5. Prepare epoxy resin according to kit instructions, careful to mix evenly and carefully.
6. Pour the prepared resin into the silicone molds to create "eomija" (어미자) characters.
7. Allow for resin to cure for 24-48 hours.
8. Once the eomija characters are cured, remove from the silicone mold, and inspect for imperfections.
9. Clean silicone from the resin eomija characters.
10. Place the completed resin types in the correct order for future use.

Printing

1. Obtain a flat sheet of aluminum and arrange the resin characters in the correct order.
2. Using melted beeswax, adhere each individual resin type to the flat surface.
3. Once completed, double check for the correct order.
4. Acquire ink or paint and lightly brush over resin types.
5. Obtain Hanji paper and lay flat on top of resin types, using a block press down paper onto resin types and rub over the surface to imprint the paper.
6. Remove Hanji and let it dry.
7. Repeat for desired copies.

Discussion of Results

While the resources I had from detailed images and a written process illuminated me on how to proceed with the initial carving steps, I was mostly in the dark for how the rest of the procedure would unfold with the liquid silicone and epoxy resin substitutions I made due to contemporary inaccessibility to other items.[19] It is within this section that I will dissect the shortcomings of technical writings and the mental map of previous experience through the reworking of this experiment.

---

[19] For images depicting the beeswax carving portion please see: Pow-Key Sohn, 1982. *Early Korean typography*. Seoul: Po Chin Chai.

Figure 1: First Character Carved out of Beeswax. 無 (wu2, simplified 无) Black ink has been placed on top to ease the identification of the craft. (Moreno, 2022)

Carving Process

For the first section of my project, I utilized cosmetic level beeswax to carve out the initial molds for the experiment. While wax is known to be flexible and easily imprinted, I did not foresee the ease with which the wax's properties would vary depending on my handling. The advantages of wax are many, for example the moldability allows for intricate designs even on a smaller level that are sometimes lost to us in other materials and the possibility to restart in the case of an error. However, there are a couple of disadvantages to also keep in mind. Wax's properties change depending on the temperature of the environment, beeswax has a relatively higher melting point than most other waxes at 62° C but any change in the environment can cause it to soften. In my process of carving, I experienced difficulty with the first character 無 (wu2, simplified 无) shown in figure 1 due to the toughness of the wax itself. It required much more force in order to successfully carve out the exterior of the mold, in order to combat this problem, I filled a cup with hot water and dipped my metal carving tools into water before drying and attempting to carve the wax again. The rise in temperature of the metal allowed for the wax to be imprinted easier and eliminated the issue of exerting more force and losing control for the precision of certain detailing in the mold. While one problem had been successfully resolved with an increase in contact temperature, another arose. During the carving of the latter characters, there was an increase in the ease for the carving tool to shape the wax which caused a reanalysis of the amount of force used to carve into the wax. I hypothesize that this was a direct result from the heat transferred from my hands to the wax itself. In order to address this new issue, I would place the wax blocks into my freezer to allow for the wax's temperature to cool prior to resuming the carving process.

While I had never carved anything out of wax prior to this experiment, the innate knowledge of wax properties and experience with candles gave way to the ease with which certain hindrances could be addressed. Within the original procedure, there is no annotated note section that contains "In case of trouble, attempt the following…" to assure that practitioners of the craft are able to navigate shortcomings. The original artisans as well as current masters of craft have committed to heart the material properties of the objects they work with, and each developed their own methods to solve arising problems. For example, one would be able to recognize that wax is an object with sliding properties as it is reliant on the surrounding temperature, whether that temperature is manipulated by the subject or the environment. According to the Accuweather weather ranges, Cheongju's current climate appears to have an even demonstration of the four seasons.[20] This would make the case that during pre-Modern times, the Buddhist monks themselves would either adapt their temples to be more conducive to their craft workshops. I conducted my experiment during the Spring in a closed environment with no heat or air conditioning, allowing me to maintain the surrounding environment relatively neutral at around 22° C separate from the rest of the world. Through this portion of the experiment, I was able to take note not only of the initial wax models and the level of knowledge required for their creation, but also the contributing factors surrounding the atmosphere.

Casting Techniques

The entirety of this section within the procedure was adapted to best-fit my accessibility to resources based on location as well as skill set. Throughout the liquid silicone molding process, the instructions indicated that one needed to set the molds on the bottom of a container and pour over the mixture. One immediate reaction to this action was the wax models floating to the top of the liquid silicone instead of staying steadfast to the bottom, in order to combat for the liquid silicone mixture being denser than the wax models, I took tweezers and flipped over the molds so that they would be flat base up and the actual character face down. My concern while doing this was that the models would eventually sink into the silicone. However, after monitoring for an hour after the initial pour, I

---

[20] "Cheongju Weather" Accuweather, accessed April 20, 2022,
https://www.accuweather.com/en/kr/cheongju/223115/

noticed that the models were staying in place and the molds were curing as expected. My liquid silicone instruction booklet suggested placing the solution in a refrigerator at 17° C to help with the curing process. After placing the container in the appropriate environment, I left it to cure and set for 48 hours.

I will acknowledge that for the majority of this step, I was utilizing my own tacit knowledge using liquid silicone and epoxy resin for smaller crafts instead of going off of previous scholarship that utilized molten metal to create exact replicas. After the initial 48-hour period had passed, the mold was mostly cured. However, I noticed that there was still more residue remaining over the wax models. In order to attempt and resolve this issue, the mold was allowed to rest for an additional day. After the initial attempt at addressing this curing issue, I removed the models and left it to air dry alone. The removal of the wax did not aid the molds. It appears that I overlooked the chemical interactions between organic materials (wax) and inorganic materials (liquid silicone). After doing some research on liquid silicone, I simply used water to wash away any sticky residue from the sections that had not solidified due to the contact with wax. I wanted to attempt to pour the epoxy resin in order to get a final product despite the initial mishap with the silicone mold and not having enough time to switch the substitution itself. What resulted was an entire mess, the resin was unable to cure, and the existing molds were rendered unusable due to the resin. This halted the experiment according to the original plan written above. In order to remain with the integrity of the project and experiment, I decided to utilize my wax models as the final printing typefaces.

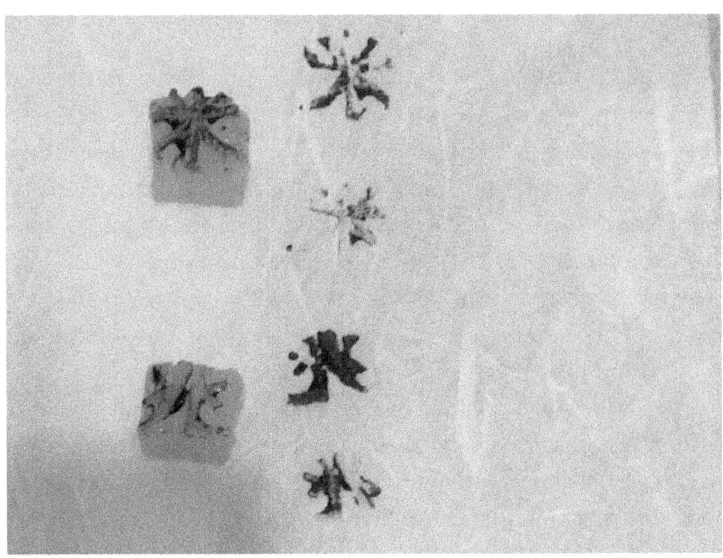

Figure 2: Two wax model characters and their accompanying ink prints. (Moreno, 2022)

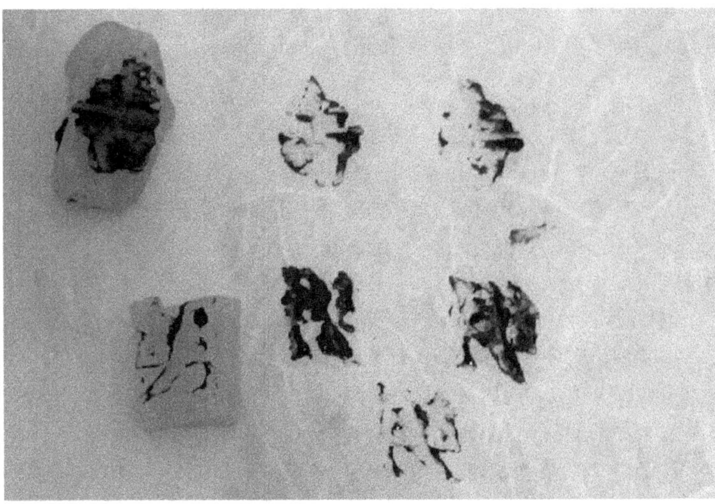

Figure 3: Two wax model characters and their ink prints emphasis on outlines. (Moreno, 2022).

Printing Procedure

Due to a lack of a resin typeface, I used my original wax models as printing material. While I was unable to directly observe the texture of the resin typeface, I was able to still obtain printed characters from the wax models themselves. Below in *Figure* 2 you can observe the prints of a couple different characters. Beeswax is not typically used as an imprinting material, as mentioned previously the texture and characteristics of the wax itself were interesting and beneficial during the initial carving procedure for its flexibility and ability to regroup after a possible carving error. However, for the printing procedure there were several things that stood out during the process. First of all, it was relatively easy to attach the typefaces themselves to the aluminum sheet since the wax was all the same. When it came to the actual transfer of the character, there were varying degrees of printing. Not all characters transferred over equally, some left deeper imprints than others or some simply had an outline of the character as emphasized in *Figure 3.* After the ink rubbing was done, I examined the wax models to take in any change in the physical shape. The characters appeared to be flatter than they were prior to the printing. The wax models were unintentionally modified due to the pressure from the ink rubbing, this result explains why craftsmen typically removed themselves from using flexible organic materials towards the metal type that wore off slower through the labor induced ink printing.

Woodblock prints, while solid and useful for many copies also had a similar problem like the wax models because multiple prints would wear off the etching and the imprints would vary the more copies that were made. While copper and iron typefaces were not safe from the eroding effects of printing, they still stood a longer chance at preserving their original forms than wood, clay, or wax. Another oversight during the printing process was the revelation that a couple of my characters when printed were backwards! Despite my best attempts at following my instructions to a tee, I overlooked a couple of the characters by carving them out normally rather than reverse. I adjusted the characters and was able to print them the correct way. Other observations from the printing process that correlated with previous scholarship and the *Jikji* manuscript included the variation in which aspects of characters showed up more prominent and had different emphasis on what portions could be identifiable. Of course, a couple of the character's faults were from the initial wax carving process and had nothing to do with the printing process. Following through this process, I could not help but wonder what aspects of the characters would have been lost in-between the molding and resin curing process and how the original artisans combated this issue.

Would it have been easier to carve the characters deeper into the small blocks of wax or making the typefaces themselves larger?

All in all, the ability to move within the space as an observer and as the practitioner granted me a new perspective into the materiality of the typeface itself as well as a new perspective into the world of the craftsmen.

Applications of Rework Methodology

Rework methodology does not only allow historians to rewrite the history of objects, but it also grants a new frame of understanding for the intimate knowledge lost to the passing of time. To some, a reinterpretation of an experiment that has already been conducted can appear to be futile and a waste of time. However, there is a richness to the reinterpretation of an item in a different setting. As demonstrated throughout this paper, the aim of this project is to recreate the technology in order to attempt to consolidate the innate knowledge that was unearthed from the bottom of one's mind to achieve a clear end goal.

It was extremely difficult to attempt and estimate the amount of time this entire project would take from start to finish. What I assumed would be nothing more than 72 hours due to all of the substitutions that were made to facilitate the execution, ended up being a total of one week. I had not expected the carving to take as long as it did. Within my original proposal of this project, I wanted to replicate an entire page from the *Jikji* that encompassed 180-200 total characters. This would prove itself ambitious as it took me about 7-15 minutes per character, depending on my familiarity with it and where I was within the process of familiarizing myself with my tools and materials. When I made a small mistake, that of carving characters in the opposite orientation, I knew that I would be unable to carve the total sum and resigned myself to 30 characters, which still took 2 entire days. The rest of the process was extensive due to the time periods that liquid silicone and epoxy resin require to cure and set. As I went along, I modified the amount of work that I did in order to meet my deadline, however I would love to possibly recreate this experiment to its full capacity in the near future.

Within the realm of rework, Pamela Smith has indoctrinated herself and her initiative "The Making and Knowing Project: Intersections of Craft Making and

Scientific Knowledge."[21] This project engages readers to take on the feat of decoding technical writing and artisanal craft knowledge. While her work is essential to the overall academic field, it lacks some diversity. The scope of her initiative focuses on the Western primary source BnF Ms. Fr. 640, a unique manuscript testifying to the widespread of art and crafts from the 16th century.[22] It is from her initiative and students that I was able to frame this project within a manner that allowed for extrapolation of a combination in scientific method and humanitarian research to contribute to material associating the artisanal craft knowledge of Asia to that of the European world. Primary, I want to bring to attention the work of Suzanne B. Butters whose dive into the 16th century art of Italy brought about an ekphrasis to create a tangible form of a skill and that when skill is repeated through a course of various works it can be acknowledged as wisdom.[23] From this I attribute that that empirical knowledge precedes an artist/craftsman when creating a new work of art, but the response of unforeseen material anomalies when producing art is what ties together what we see as artisanal knowledge and allows us to describe the material culture of an item in regard to its legacy and history.

Conclusion

While my recreation did not execute a final product, it did provide me with more context when reviewing previous scholarship and analyzing contemporary materials and their contribution to this section of scholarship. I set out to examine the effect that metal moveable type had not only on the individuals that created it but also on the rest of the world and its subsequent followers. While metal printing did not take off in East Asia as profoundly as it did in the West, the establishment of an office dedicated strictly to developing typefaces and moveable metal types are still impressive feats demonstrated by the Korean people in the 14th century and beyond.

---

[21] See more about Professor Pamela Smith's initiative at Columbia University at: https://www.makingandknowing.org

[22] Interestingly enough, it is housed in the same library as the Jikji!

[23] Suzanne B. Butters, "From Skills to Wisdom Making, Knowing, and the Arts" in *Ways of making and knowing: the material culture of empirical knowledge*, ed. Pamela H. Smith, Amy R. W. Meyers, and Harold J. Cook. (Ann Arbor: University of Michigan Press, 2017) 48-85.

Language and the Written Word

Language allows us humans to communicate with others, convey our thoughts, and create the unthinkable. With language, literacy has closely followed as we turned from a society of mental skill and knowledge to one of written documentation. For the Koryŏ dynasty monks, their primary motivation of the period was to spread the word of Sŏn Buddhism (Zen Buddhism) and to do so, they printed various books detailing the words and practices of Buddha to disseminate their word to others. It was through a combination of previous skill working with iron and bronze and the power of literacy that gave way to the first metal moveable type in the world. Once this artisanal skill is removed from its function, we can explore its impact on the rest of society. For example, these monks were well educated in written Classical Chinese and held the capacity to identify and write these characters freely, they used this skill set to translate it over to both woodblock print and moveable type print as well. Their knowledge of the characters' properties allowed them to realize that in order to print, one would have to mirror the character prior to carving. It is within these small details that innate knowledge resides. For example, when taking a look at the wax models, the models themselves measured approximately 1 cm x 1 cm, which allowed for a very small working area. The thought of having to intricately carve out individual characters, some more complicated than others served a hefty feat. I have studied Chinese for the past 6-8 years and regard myself to have the familiarity necessary for reading and writing simplified Sino-characters, I will note that the Buddhist monks first in charge of carving out characters from either wax models or into wooden prints had double or triple the amount of familiarity and knowledge with characters having gone through school and they themselves memorized various scripts full of the teachings of the Buddha that they then went on to copy and print to spread. Similarly, individuals throughout the Chosŏn dynasty also received a great deal of education in the classics and a large portion of their education focused on the ability for them to master calligraphy and reading of classical Chinese. I believe that these initial steps that led to the familiarity of the characters allowed for these craftsmen to become knowledgeable carvers just as much as calligraphers and allowed them to recognize the motion of the characters just as much as the simple function of carving. Surely, these years of reinforced skill allowed for a process of mental recognition that could not be transcribed into technical writings.

Tacit Knowledge

As noted earlier in the results and discussion section of the essay, while the results of the experiment were underwhelming in terms of creating an adequate end product. The process through which I as an experimenter and empiricist undertook was nothing short of a real success. It is through those moments that knowledge appears to run thin that new ideas are developed, and the extent of the troubleshooting mind is highlighted. As inherent scientists and explorers of the unknown, humans go through life acquiring new skills left and right but never pausing to reflect where exactly that information gets stored within the mind. Going through the phases of life becomes routine and our motor skills are second nature. However, as time and generations go by, an individual's mental bank for skills that we consider crafts does not seem to change as much as we initially suspect. There is an in-between written knowledge and mental knowledge that automatically gets filled when doing certain items that you may not realize until you have the ability to sit down and deeply think about things. For example, in our modern-day contemporary we use technology to identify temperatures and have various numbers that are "correct" for different things such as toasting, baking, etc. Our predecessors functioned perfectly without the technology to place numbers to procedures and simply learned to tell apart different flame sizes, the materials that would make a certain flame stronger, and other methods we do not look for today due to the ease of simply using a number temperature and going with it. No matter how much reading you do about certain skills, the actual practice of it is what gets you far.

Overall naivety that this experiment would go without a hitch in the plan left me without an expected end result. However, I was still able to quickly think of alternatives to check the success of my carving through other means. This project has been a wonderful learning experience in terms of combating personal assumptions and confidences that ultimately led to small hiccups along the way. Literacy and language are both still ever present in today's world as we learn to create new ways to disseminate our thoughts with the new world. In our contemporary world, we are currently used to writing and typing on our electronic devices and utilizing the internet to transfer information from one source to another. The questions are still the same, how do we facilitate the process for spreading knowledge? What can we do to minimize the errors and mistakes? What method is the most cost-effective? We may be living in a different time with new technologies, however, we as humans battle some of the same obstacles just in different forms. It is said that history repeats itself, what's to say that human thinking does not do the same?

Acknowledgements

This paper and experiment came about as a part of Washington University in St. Louis' Spring 2022 courses Kitchen, Studio, Factory: Making in East Asia and Nature, Technology, and Medicine in Korea led by Dr. Hyeok Hweon Kang. It was thanks to his dedication to rework methodology and holistic approach to materiality and artisanal culture that such a work as this could come about to see the world. For more information on this project and for others in the field of rework methodology please check out:

https://www.kitchenstudiofactory.com/rework-project/

The Entangled History of the Korean Semiconductor Industry: Between Imitation and Innovation, Central and Peripheral, Research and Production

Gunwoo Lee

Abstract

In 2019, 17.9% of the total value of products exported from Korea were semiconductors.[1] Before the 1970s, however, Korea didn't have a semiconductor manufacturing industry. Instead, the country's manufacturers relied on semiconductors fabricated from Japan and the United States to build their consumer electronics. The same was true for most other regions outside of the United States, Japan and Europe, as the three countries comprised 99% of the total semiconductors manufactured worldwide.[2]

---

[1] Korea Customs Service, p'ummokpyŏl such'uripsiljŏk [Export and Import based on items], https://unipass.customs.go.kr/ets/index.do?menuId=ETS_MNU_00000103

[2] Semiconductor History Museum of Japan, 1970, *Scale of the global semiconductor market is 870 billion yen*, Trends in the semiconductor Industry, 1970s, https://www.shmj.or.jp/english/trends/trd70s.html

After the 1970s, however, the industry experienced a dramatic shift. Japan quickly expanded its market share and soon after, Korea began to dominate the memory portion of semiconductor production. This paper will attempt to explain the sudden shift by postulating that the transmission of knowledge in the semiconductor industry occurs through a complicated web of collaboration, copying, and reverse engineering.

The beginning of the Korean Semiconductor Industry

During the U.S led semiconductor hegemony of the early 1970s, Dr. Kang Ki-dong created the first semiconductor company in Korea called Korea Semiconductor. While the company was new compared to early competitors such as Motorola, General Electric, or Fairchild, their products weren't far behind global standards. Indeed, in less than two years after establishment, Korea Semiconductor rolled out its first product using the CMOS (complementary metal-oxide-semiconductor) transistor, a state-of-the-art technology at the time.[3] How was this possible in such a short time?

Kang's expertise in the semiconductor business stems from his long career in the U.S semiconductor industry. After graduating from Seoul National University with a degree in electrical engineering, he attended Missouri State University for a few months and transferred to Ohio State University. At Ohio State University, he was asked to join a new semiconductor lab, which required him to shift his previous specialty from electrical engineering to semiconductors fabrication. His prolific academic career led him to Motorola in 1962, where he organized a team of engineers involved in building fabrication processes. The long career in Motorola and a short stint at Stuart Warner soon ended when Kang decided to create his own business in Korea.

After receiving a million-dollar fund from Kim Kyu Han, president of KEMCO, Kang created the Korea Semiconductor in 1974. Kang already had experience setting up production when he was ordered to direct a project of building a new plant in Korea while at Motorola. With his experience, it took him only a year and a half to complete his factory in Puch'ŏn, where he started producing chips for electronic watches.[4]

---

[3] chŏnja sigye yangsan, maeil gyŏngje, September 29, 1975

[4] Gang, Gidong. *Gang Gidong Gwa Hanguk Bandoche.* (Seoul: Amoreu Mundi, 2018), 222

In building his factory, Kang describes the process as follows :

> *The patterns, or masks, we were buying from the U. S., so it was the same thing. The wafers we were buying from [the] U. S., so the same thing. And the equipment, I had a hundred percent of it purchased from the U.S. because that was the equipment I knew. All right, so it's [the] same equipment. The only difference is the people running it.*[5]

Some might describe it as a direct form of copying. Indeed, in a literal sense, Kang copied the equipment, the material used, and the know-how, from the United States back into Korea. Is this form of coping, which is not even a form of reverse-engineering, a direct opposition to innovation? To unravel the seemingly adversarial relationship, we will first examine the start and development of the semiconductor business from a glocalized perspective. Through both the established and marginal history of semiconductors, we glimpse a complex, interconnected relationship between centers and peripheries, between imitation and innovation, that defies the conventional knowledge associated with the nomenclature.

Between Research and Manufacturing

Semiconductor manufacturing is and has been, a heavily research-oriented and costly business. In 2019, R&D amounted to more than 14.2% of global semiconductor revenue[6], and the investment cost of building a leading-edge-fabrication facility averages between 15 to 20 billion dollars.[7] Most of the costs related to building fabrication facilities are directly invested in to equipment that requires years of research and development. One example of this is the EUV(extreme ultraviolet) lithography machine from ASML, which is essential in the pattern drawing process of leading fabrication facilities. ASML's EUV started its development in the 1990s and began commercial production in the late 2010s, costing over 7 billion dollars in R&D until 2014 with a price tag of $150 million

---

[5] Ki Dong Kang, interview by Andrew GoldStein, June 13, 1996, interview 270, IEEE History Center, Picataway, NJ

[6] McLean & Company, *The McClean Report 2022*, January 2022

[7] Nicolas Mokhoff, "Semi Industry Fab Costs Limit Industry Growth," *EE Times*, March 10, 2012

per machine.[8] [9] In the trend of semiconductors, we see a prioritization of research and cumulation of technology over expenses such as marketing. Even mass production, which was previously seen as a separate department, is closely intertwined with research, as manufacturing production lines are routinely converted into research facilities and vice versa. However, such a close-knit relationship isn't limited to research and production inside the company. We observe a non-linear, non-individualistic progression of knowledge through a complicated cross-network of research and production between companies as well.

Bell Labs, a research institute located in the United States, were the first to come up with early concepts of semiconductors such as the first transistor (point contact transistor) in 1947, the first Bipolar transistor in 1948, and the first MOSFET transistor in 1959. The concepts were quickly adapted by the early contenders in the semiconductor market like Texas Instruments, General Electric, Fairchild Semiconductor, and Motorola[10], who were keen on imitating these ideas and actualizing them into reality. In the semiconductor industry, the focus was not on the origin of an idea, but the process of adaptation and realization of the idea through manufacturing. However, not all concepts originated from a single point. Alloy transistor by General Electric and the Planar transistor by Fairchild influenced the research at bell labs and vice versa. By examining the semiconductor industry in its infancy, we observe an interconnected web of reciprocal transmission of knowledge between research and manufacturing.

However, the interconnection of research and manufacturing are not limited to an industry. Individuals like Kang Ki-dong also exemplifies the fusion of research and manufacturing. After the Korean War, Kang was primarily involved in amateur radios, also known as HAM radio. He would work hands-on in soldering the resistors on the transceivers. With many of his fellow friends in high school, he created the Korean Amateur Radio League – KARL in 1955, which is still in operation as of 2022.[11] With his expertise in radios and electronics, he studied electrical engineering at Seoul National University. After graduating from Seoul

---

[8] Mark Lapedus, "Billions And Billions Invested," *Semiconductor Engineering*, April 17, 2014.

[9] "Our History - Supplying the Semiconductor Industry," ASML, accessed May 3, 2022, https://www.asml.com/en/company/about-asml/history.

[10] Andrew J Butrica, "NASA's Role in the Manufacture of Integrated Circuits," in *Historical Studies in the Societal Impact of Spaceflight*, ed. Steven J Dick (NASA, n.d.), pp. 149-250.

[11] Yoo, Sangwoon, and Dongwon JO. "From Walkie-Talkie to Radio Receiver:an Entangled History of Electronic Technological Culture and the Beginning of Semiconductor Industry." *The Korean Jornal of History of Science* 43, no. 3 (2021): 557–600. https://doi.org/10.36092/kjhs.2021.43.3.557.

National University and entering Ohio State University for graduate school, he joined the new semiconductor lab as a researcher. While he was a prolific researcher in Solid State Diffusion, as the first staff in the lab, he was also involved in the process of acquiring equipment, setting up the lab, and hiring[12].

The logistical experience at the semiconductor lab in Ohio was essential when he was asked to lead a research team at Motorola. Compared to IBM and Fairchild, Motorola lacked a significant research division. Kang started by hiring researchers and workers from the manufacturing line and incorporating them into his research team.[13] He then worked on procuring equipment for the research line. In the process, he would salvage leading-edge production equipment that had been discarded due to low capacity and convert it for research. After setting up the pilot lines, the manufacturing processes from the research team were selectively adapted to the mass production lines. In his later years at Motorola, he was also involved in setting up production facilities in Hongkong and Korea. However, he wasn't solely focused on manufacturing logistics in Motorola. He was also a researcher at heart, developing the radiation-hardened semiconductor for the pentagon[14] and the ground-isolation method for vibration damping.[15]

Following the history of the semiconductor industry, we see that the dichotomy between research and manufacturing can be blurred. Manufacturing equipment such as lithography machines requires research as much as the scientific background of semiconductors themselves. Then how is the entanglement of research and manufacturing important in explaining the birth of the semiconductor in Korea? Research, in its nominal form, are center of knowledge and is often characterized as an innovator as it creates new knowledge. Manufacturing, on the other hand, are often characterized as peripheries, as mass production utilizes the knowledge created through research, and is often described as imitators. Through semiconductors, however, we see that both research and manufacturing are generators, and end-users of knowledge that affect each other reciprocally. If this is true, we need to re-establish the concept of centers and peripheries and question if innovation and imitation are entangled concepts as well.

---

[12] Gang, Gidong. "Gang Gidong Gwa Hanguk Bandoche," 124

[13] *IBID*, 134~140

[14] *IBID*, 10~21

[15] *IBID*, 149~153

Center and Peripheries

Transmission of knowledge occurs through imitation

Compared to Japan and the United States in the 1970s and 1980s, Korea can be considered a periphery in the Semiconductor industry. Before Kang's establishment of the Korean Semiconductor in 1973, Anam Electronics was the only semiconductor company in Korea. Though Anam was technically a semiconductor company, it was only involved in manufacturing the header of the semiconductor – a plastic case wrapping the outer shell of the semiconductor. Thus, when Kang came back to Korea for his semiconductor business in 1973, the technological background in Korea was non-existent. To compensate for the apparent lack of infrastructure, Kang copied the process and equipment he used during his time at Motorola in building his factories.

However, we need to have a much more contextualized view of the process. The Korean semiconductor industry at the time was much different than the already ripe industry in the United States. In the 1970s, the concept of semiconductors manufacturing in Korea was limited to packing technology. The import and export codes for semiconductor equipment did not exist, and Semiconductor businesses were met with red tapes as rules and regulations classifying the industry did not exist. To make it worse, due to the oil shock of 1973, Korea did not have a consistent supply of electricity [16] and the time frame for transportation of equipment was stretched. As a result, Kang had to go to the United States multiple times to ship equipment on commercial flights as in-flight luggage [17].

While Kang's manufacturing process was not much different from those in the United States, the implementation was vastly different. The semiconductor industry in the United States went through extensive support from the government such as contracts from the military. Korea did not have governmental aid during this period as compared to countries such as the United States or Japan. When Kang submitted his business proposal to the officials, the government refused to sign the proposal until further technical review, as semiconductors in Korea during in the 1970s were only defined in terms of packing technology. As a result, the Korean semiconductor industry was not a simple copy and paste of the technology from the United States. Rather, it had to go through a series of

---

[16] Jŏngsuk Kim, yegoŏmnŭn 停電(chŏngjŏn) chaja, Chosun Ilbo, September 9, 1974

[17] Gang, Gidong. *Gang Gidong Gwa Hanguk Bandoche*, 124

independent development and resolutions. As such, we need to contextually differentiate the two industries.

Peripheries affect centers

In 1975, Samsung Electronics took over Korea Semiconductor. The equipment and personnel were incorporated into the electronics giant and became the seeds of what is now the biggest semiconductor manufacturer in the world. Samsung, which can be characterized as a center of knowledge by Kim Linsu's definition,[18] shifted its whole business to Semiconductors after the takeover and was able to quickly catch up to the global semiconductor standards.

During the 1990s, when Samsung was still a contender in the semiconductor industry, and the memory industry was divided into DDR DRAM and RDRAM. Samsung placed its main emphasis on researching DDR DRAM technology.[19] The bet proved to be wildly successful, and Samsung's DDR DRAM technology became the global standard, putting Samsung at the top of the memory business.

As Korea Semiconductor, a periphery in the semiconductor industry became the seedling of Samsung's semiconductor venture, we see that peripheries can also become centers of knowledge as the knowledge generated from the periphery can be adapted into the centers.

Imitation and Innovation

Now let's go back to examining the relationship between innovation and imitation. We have postulated that in terms of research and manufacturing, centers and peripheries do not exist separately. As such, we have questioned the need to evaluate whether innovation and imitation cannot exist separately since research and manufacturing can be explained through innovation and imitation.

---

[18] Linsu Kim, Imitation to Innovation: The Dynamics of Korea's Technological Learning (New York: ACLS History E-Book Project, 2005).

[19] Omun'gil, 4pae pparŭn 'singk'ŭringk'ŭDraem' kaebal, maeil kyŏngje, November 4, 1997

Yoo and Cho[20][21][22] believe that at the beginning of the semiconductor industry in Korea, the industry went through a period of multifaceted entanglement. They claim that the bloom of the semiconductor industry was a result of the entanglement of knowledge and execution, technology and culture, amateur and professional, civilian and military, official and non-officials. Such entanglement, as Yoo postulates, can be described as a web of different ideas and concepts that link together to form something new.

Intuitively, imitation cannot exist without innovation as something needs to be created to be imitated. Counter-intuitively, innovation cannot exist without imitation, as every product needs to have a background and a foundation upon which the product is built. Semiconductors, which are thought to be an "innovative product", are based upon technologies such as electricity, conductors, or vacuum tubes. While we need to prove that there is no such thing as 'pure' innovation, if pure innovation does not exist, then imitation and innovation cannot exist without the other. In other words, innovations are based upon imitation, and imitations are based upon innovation. In explaining this relationship, the paper will propose a drastic idea: that imitation and innovation are essentially the same. As Yoo and Cho claim, imitative products can also be described as innovative, and innovative products can also be called imitative. If innovation is also based upon something else, the only difference, one could propose, is the degree to which a new product diverges from the object that it derives from. However, differentiating innovation and imitation based on the degree of divergence is subjective. Thus, if innovation and imitation are subjective terms, innovation and imitation are indistinguishable in nature.

---

[20] Yoo, Sangwoon, and Dongwon JO. "From Walkie-Talkie to Radio Receiver:an Entangled History of Electronic Technological Culture and the Beginning of Semiconductor Industry." *The Korean Jornal of History of Science* 43, no. 3 (2021): 557–600. https://doi.org/10.36092/kjhs.2021.43.3.557.

[21] Yoo, Sangwoon. "Innovation in Practice: The 'Technology Drive Policy' and the 4mb DRAM R&D Consortium in South Korea in the 1980s and 1990s." *Technology and Culture* 61, no. 2 (2020): 385–415. https://doi.org/10.1353/tech.2020.0047.

[22] Jo, Dongwon. "Vernacular Technical Practices beyond the Imitative/Innovative Boundary: Apple II Cloning in Early-1980s South Korea." *East Asian Science, Technology and Society: An International Journal*, 2021, 1–24. https://doi.org/10.1080/18752160.2021.1962616.

Copying and imitation

If innovation and imitation are indistinguishable terms, how can we explain the direct copy of the U.S. manufacturing process by Korea Semiconductor? As we have described above, even direct copies can be contextually differentiated from the original product. In the global semiconductor industry, the manufacturing process has been a close network of collaboration, imitation, and direct copying. Products and their manufacturing process are sometimes indistinguishable. However, the implementation of production can be vastly different.

In the race for smaller transistor sizes in the current semiconductor industry, while semiconductor companies reach the same transistor size, the process of reaching the same goal were different. In the development of the same 7nm manufacturing process node of Samsung and TSMC, Samsung utilized EUV, while TSMC utilized DUV with multi-patterning. Likewise, companies have strived towards achieving the same structural concepts such as MOSFET, CMOS, or more currently, GAA. With the same processing nodes and structural designs, the resulting products are sometimes indistinguishable and are often compatible with each other. However, companies go through different process of research and development.

In a similar context, the transmission of semiconductor technology in Korea underwent a different process from the rise of semiconductors in the United States. Though the manufacturing process of semiconductors was essentially the same, the implementation differentiates the two industries. We observe that a direct copy can diverge from the original product in a more contextualized view. If we accept that innovation and imitation are essentially the same, then we can conclude that the start of the semiconductor industry in Korea is distinguishable from the semiconductor industry of the United States and is both imitative and innovative.

Conclusion

The start of the semiconductor industry in Korea occurred through a direct copy of the semiconductor industry in the United States. However, the semiconductor industry is a complex network of collaboration, imitation, and direct copying. We can apply the framework and explain that the transmission of semiconductor knowledge from the United States to Korea also occurs through a similar process.

In the history of semiconductors, research and manufacturing are both generators of knowledge that transmit knowledge bidirectionally. If we use the conventional definition of center and periphery and characterize research as centers of knowledge and manufacturing as peripheries, centers and peripheries can both become generators of knowledge. While the term center and periphery might be necessary to explain one instance of transmission of knowledge, it would be difficult to identify a certain area of industry as centers or peripheries.

Through the relationship between centers and peripheries, we observe that imitation and innovation are not only reciprocal but indistinguishable. In the history of technology, both imitation and innovation are based on something else. While some might argue that innovation is distinct from imitation as there is a bigger divergence between object or idea that is based upon, we believe that such distinction is subjective and blurry.

Finally, copies and original products in the semiconductor industry can be differentiated by examining the process of transmission. The direct copying of semiconductor technology from the United States to Korea underwent a separate process of resolution with societal and cultural factors. If we blur the lines between innovation and imitation, then the transmission of semiconductor technology in Korea does not directly oppose our understanding of innovation.

Why Stubbornly Pseudoscience? Continuing Presence of Powerful Divination in South Korea

Tony Kwon

Abstract

Science has provided an antidote to a world full of uncertainty and instability; it has not only impressed society with its various technological innovations and monumental achievements to make the world more connected, but it has also brought the pleasure of convenience, efficiency, and accuracy to everyday life. Interestingly, the rather technologically sophisticated state of South Korea stubbornly utilizes the field of pseudoscience, which includes the practices of divination and various forms of fortune-telling techniques. These divinatory practices, including Four Pillar Destiny, physiognomy, tarot, and others have been integrated within pop culture for such a long time that there are reportedly more than 300,000 divination practitioners, with market value at more than $3.7 billion in the Korean economy today.[1] Though there are those who view divination as disjointed from their daily lives, a sizable portion of the Korean population views divination as pertinent to their existence. In this paper, I will thus examine changes within the divination system and the strategic presence of its niche market from

---

[1] Kim, David J. "Four Pillars and Four Diviners: Fate, Fluidity, and Invention in Horoscopic Saju Divination in Contemporary South Korea." Journal of Korean Religions, Volume 10, Number 2, October 2019, pp. 301-329. https://doi.org/10.1353/jkr.2019.0007

the early Chosun period to modern Korea. Through this historical inquiry, I will further delve into the bilateral relationship between divination and contemporary society.

Introduction

What comes to your mind first when you think of South Korea? The empire of semiconductors? The producer of cutting-edge smartphones? Perhaps the highly safe surveillance state with closed-circuit television (CCTV) cameras that eliminate "perfect crime" in public? In fact, South Korea has been known as a scientifically and technologically thriving society. However, a significant number of South Koreans are still highly intertwined with what one might call 'pseudoscience.' Pseudoscience is often defined as a subject in which its system of explanation and method involving theories resembling that of genuine science but cannot be empirically supported due to faulty premises and falsifiability.[2] The modern scientific community dismissed this superstition that lacks both empirical evidence and scientific approach. Thus, divination is considered pseudoscience since its approach is mistakenly regarded as scientific. In fact, this form of pseudoscience has been categorized as neither science nor religion yet continues to be deeply rooted in Korean culture. Many Koreans practice and partake in divination, arguably the most dominant strand of Korean pseudoscience. Consider, for example, the recent presidential candidate Yoon Seok Yeol who appeared with the 'king' (王) sign on his left palm during the presidential election debate and was eventually elected as 20th president of South Korea. Soon, the online debate unexpectedly shifted to a back-and-forth exchange over local shamanistic beliefs and the media began to question the power and social acceptance of fortune-telling.[3] Also, if you walk along the commercially booming streets of Seoul, you can effortlessly find fortune teller booths, shops, and even cafes where people, regardless of their age and gender, visit to see their future for entertainment purpose or critical life guidance.

---

[2] Ellerton, Peter. "Where Is the Proof in Pseudoscience?" The Conversation, 24 Mar. 2022, https://theconversation.com/where-is-the-proof-in-pseudoscience-22184.

[3] "Ending Shamanism in Politics." Korea JoongAng Daily. Accessed March 31, 2022. https://koreajoongangdaily.joins.com/2022/01/19/opinion/editorials/Yoon-Sukyeol shamanism/20220119194656558.html.

South Koreans indeed have been using numerous fortune-telling subjects such as *saju myŏngni* ("Four Pillar Destiny"), shamanism, horoscopy, astrology, physiognomy, palmistry, tarot, chiromancy, necromancy, geomancy, and so forth to predict one's future. Within such a large spectrum of Korean fortune telling methods, I use the term divination to refer holistically to all fortune telling subjects in this paper. Since *saju* is one of the most common and fundamental divination techniques, I emphasize this practice, examining how diviners have been shaping and shaped by Korean society.

Despite being a technologically sophisticated society, pseudoscientific practices are extremely prevalent in South Korea, specifically divination, ranging from *saju* to folk religion.[4] In this paper, I argue that divination has become socially viable in Korea because South Korean divination communities 1) led a smooth transition on adjusting their theoretical framework from the early to modern concerns within the broadened scope of patrons, 2) built a solid niche market that encourages competition, innovation, and even cooperation with government within a culturally institutionalized environment, and 3) strategically set an atmosphere where its communication style influences divination patrons to be epistemically negligent. In doing so, I will first provide the historical backdrop regarding oscillating presence of divination communities, what the divination meant for early Korea, and how its old-fashioned techniques are different from modern divination models as well as how its changes have bilaterally interacted with Korean society. In my analysis, I will not only delve into historical traces of why divination itself is so variable to time and space but also explore societal, cultural, and cognitive factors to explain why and how the divination communities have well managed to flourish in techno-savvy South Korea. Furthermore, I hope to take an open perspective in my analysis in acknowledging the legitimate possibility of divination and other forms of pseudoscience.

Historical backdrop

What is Divination and How does it work?

Historically speaking, divinatory practices were originally derived from two dominant traditions in South Korea: *sinjŏm* (신점) conducted by a *mudang* (무당)

---

[4] Perkins, McKenzie. "What Is Folk Religion?" Learn Religions, Learn Religions, 25 June 2019, https://www.learnreligions.com/folk-religion-4588370.

and *yŏksul* (역술) conducted by a *yŏksulga* (역술가).[5] In fact, *saju* (사주) also known as Four Pillar Destiny (FPD) or *sajup'alja* (사주팔자) is a foundational divination technique that both *mudang* and *yŏksulga* partake in. To describe it briefly, the typical FPD approach uses the patron's birthtime (year as ancestor, month as parents, day as a spouse, and hour as offspring in order) to prognosticate one's personality and fortune, the *kil-hyung-hwa-pok* (길흉화복). By dint of four major Chinese FPD Classics: *yŏnhaejap'yŏng* (연해자평) from Tang and Song dynasties, *kungt'ungbogam* (궁통보감) from Ming dynasty, *chap'yŏngjinjŏn* (자평진전) from Qing dynasty, and 적천수천미 *chŏkch'ŏnsuch'ŏnmi* from Ming dynasty, the early Korean divinators were able to adapt and develop their own techniques based on the series of FPD case studies done in Tang, Song, Ming, and Qing dynasties.[6] In terms of usage, even though the application of divination techniques slightly varies depending on where diviners learned from, the most modern and theoretically consistent and valuable FPD strategies often contain the systemic use of natural matters such as Ying and Yang, five elements (fire, water, wood, metal, and earth), characteristics of seasonal changes by month and Chinese Zodiac signs to figure one's personality and perhaps compatibility with others.

Rise and Fall of Divination in Korea

Although divination still exists today, the public reputation has been heavily restricted by sociopolitical forces. In earlier periods, its popularity was such that officials at the palace often hired diviners as officials specialized in fortune-telling, predicting weather conditions, and even arresting criminals.[7] The early Koreans even believed divination to be empirical knowledge that had accumulated throughout the history of humankind. On the other hand, as Confucianism held both cultural and political hegemony in Korea, the ruling classes began restricting the divination culture. For instance, *sinjŏm* rituals, *kut* (굿), were persecuted as superstition, or *mishin* (미신). Thus, divination was not always welcomed by the public. Other historical records indicated that these traditional divinators were expelled out of the four main gates of old Seoul in the mid 15th century. Even

---

[5] Yoo, Kwang Suk Suk. "Evolutionary Adaptation of Korean Divination to Religious Markets." Asian Journal of Social Science, vol. 45, no. 4-5, 1 Jan. 2017, pp. 548–567., https://doi.org/10.1163/15685314-04504009.

[6] Kim, ch'unghyŏn. "A Study on the Temporal Characteristics of sajumyŏngnihak." kyŏnggi university yesul taehagwŏn 2018: 1-82.

[7] Yoo, "Evolutionary Adaptation," 555.

worse, since the *Kabo* Reform (1894), the village where diviners collectively resided was completely shattered by the central government in the 1930s.[8] Moreover, not all divinators were able to confidently reveal their professions to the public until the 1980s since one preeminent divinator 'foretold' the current political leader was a bad omen at that time.[9] Accordingly, politics was sometimes responsible for the diviners' displacement. For instance, former president Lee Myung-bak implemented a series of initiatives to move street diviners to designated areas, such as larger parks and outlying districts of tourist destinations in Chongno. [10] However, both the supply and demand of the divination market are still unabated. In contrast to how the government used to suppress the divination population, we're living in an era where some of the divination villages often cooperate with their municipal governments to effectively manage and maintain their presence. Today, Korean divinators are committed to being frequently and confidentially involved in the public sphere. So how can this form of pseudoscience thrive in contemporary society despite getting challenged by modern scientific communities?

From Early Modern the Modern Divination Techniques

The popularity of divination has not ceased throughout time, considering that diviners diligently devoted to a smooth adjustment of techniques suiting their modern patrons. In this segment, I will list some critical divination techniques from the past as well as modern divination models to show what kind of FPD approaches and patrons' concerns have been adjusted and prioritized, as well as how the range of patrons throughout the history has changed. As previously mentioned, the four Chinese FPD Classics had been widely recognized and used by the early and even some modern Korean diviners. Based on these four major Classics, the theoretical framework of FPD has been changed spatiotemporally. For example, consider both *yŏnhaejap'yŏng* and *kungt'ungbogam*. Out of 500 FPD cases that recorded earlier patrons' destiny, more than 300 of them are highly concerned with wealth, reputation, and bureaucratic achievement. These were therefore the top three concerns that the early patrons sought to know about their future. Particularly, the early FPD practitioners grouped these three fields as a

---

[8] *IBID.*

[9] Kim, interview.

[10] Kim, David J. "Four Pillars and Four Diviners," 309.

single matter because the only way to possess both fame and wealth was to pass the imperial examination, becoming a bureaucrat. Despite being contextualized in China, the divination techniques from the four Classics were welcomely adapted and applied by Korean diviners as the form of government and lifestyle in the early Chosun period were similar to those of China. Since the early societal structure was predominantly monarchism, achieving upward bureaucratic mobility was impossible for the underprivileged classes in both China and Korea. Thus, the early upper and middle classes were mostly applied and benefitted from the FPD method while the minorities (e.g., prostitutes, women, prisoners, and slaves) who were not treated like the upper and middle classes were socially restricted from taking the imperial exam. Today, if you have free time, with at least \$50 for the service fee in your pocket, diviners from all blocks of Seoul Street will greet you with a welcoming smile. Hence, the range of the audience has been affected by the form of society and social stratification, and this flexibility indicates that divination is not a fixed subject but necessitates a continual adjustment to one's time.

Collective Concern Vs. Individual Concern

Furthermore, *chap'yŏngjinjŏn* also emphasized a bureaucratic system where the state and society's communal concerns outweighed the individuals' concerns. For instance, most divination patrons during this period lived in agricultural society where a collective lifestyle, such as an extended family system and military troops, was often a response to questions of whether they can have prosperous agricultural seasons and win the battle against other neighboring states. Consequently, such kinds of collective concern were highly integrated with collective survivability.

However, as society began to remove these hierarchical limits and transform the ordinary lifestyle to become more democratic, individualistic, and even capitalistic, the range of audiences (divination patrons) became more diversified. So much so, in fact, that the recent theoretical framework explicitly necessitates not discriminating against the social status of patrons. Rather, the diviners were committed to embracing more kinds of patrons to effectively fulfill their curiosity. For instance, unlike the early *Chosŏn* patrons, the emergence of capitalism made this already-developed South Korea no longer problematize famine as a major concern. Regarding fortune concerns, the general problems that divinators seek to foretell branched out so that reputation, wealth, and bureaucratic achievement are now considered as individual subjects as opposed to larger groupings, and these subjects are rearranged to focus on answering individual matters in return. As a result, the demand of specified modern concerns became so in demand that

Duo, an online marriage agency, reported 82% of unmarried women and 57% of bachelors surveyed in 2017 had visited diviners to ask about romance/marital compatibility or *kung-hap* (궁합) with their prospective spouse. [11] Likewise, according to my interview with a current *mudang* Kim Taemi, recent diviners tend to focus on more differentiated future concerns such as *kung-hap*, academic achievement, and financial fortunes. These emerged and were recontextualized based on what modern patrons demanded.[12]

Birthdate Conceptualization and Religious Syncretism

One interesting feature from the past divination application is the eccentric understanding of birthdate. Although the modern FPD approaches consider the full birthdate as one's physical birth out of his or her mother's womb, one of the four major classics, *yŏnhaejap'yŏng*, follows *kit'aebŏp* (기태법), an approach that only considers the month part of one's birthdate in a newborn's FPD.[13] Since finding and applying the latter kind of birthdate would inevitably bring inaccurate fortune prediction, the former birthdate method has been universally agreed upon among diviners. Thus, the reconfiguration of the birthdate narrowed down that the specified information contributed to improve the accuracy of divination's theoretical framework.

Moreover, another spatiotemporal feature that heavily influenced the early divination system was the religious syncretism of Confucianism, Taoism, and Buddhism. As I have determined, religious beliefs and customs can be a factor in social change. This remains true for *chap'yŏngjinjŏn* and *chŏkch'ŏnsuch'ŏnmi*: both contain cases regarding the relationship between king and servants, master and apprentice, parents and children, and the distinction between male and female to convey the importance of self-cultivation and cosmic order. The authors of these classics were therefore highly influenced by Confucian beliefs of deference. In addition, the frequent mention of *t'aesikpŏp* (태식법), which refers to not only a breathing method for the fetus that is not fully developed with the nose and mouth while in their mother's womb but also one of the Taoist practices, implies the

---

[11] Park, Jun Michael. "In South Korea Fortune-Telling Will Soon Be a $3.7bn Business." The Economist. The Economist Newspaper, February 24, 2018. https://www.economist.com/asia/2018/02/24/in-south-korea-fortune-telling-will-soon-be-a-37bn-business.

[12] Kim, interview.

[13] Kim, "A Study on the Temporal Characteristics," 12

heavy influence of Taoism as well.[14] Hence, the way these practitioners engage with methods within religious frameworks and the philosophical context of these methods demonstrates that the framework of divination has long been affected by its surroundings.

Adapting Technology into Divination

Today, divination can be practiced even online. In fact, not all diviners necessarily reject genuine science nor abstain from technology. Rather, the coexistence of divination and technology brought the revolutionarily convenient divination platform. By dint of collaboration between Korean technical engineers and diviners, numerous fortune-telling *saju* software apps are now available on all our electronic devices that both diviners and patrons become more accessible to divinatory cyberspace. Downloaded over three million times, the saju app, Chomsin, provides seamless access to daily personalized fortunes. Other divinatory apps also utilize the smartphone technology of face detecting and camera technology to practice other types of divination practices such as physiognomy and palmistry.[15]

Overall, the series of evidence substantiates how the theoretical divination framework is critically sensitive to both time and space. Societal structures, such as the form of government and the understanding of specific spatiotemporal contexts, not only reconceptualize certain divination features but also broaden the range of divination patrons and the scope of societal concern to better appropriate modern times. Thus, the theoretical framework of pseudoscience (divination) is inherently flexible: this includes techniques and conceptualization of divination features. Therefore, the way diviners precisely shifted the theoretical framework, by tailoring certain fortune subjects, once broadly interlinked with others, to precisely address modern concerns, made its practice more appealing to the patrons. In doing so, they validate the omnipresence of divination to this day.

---

[14] *IBID.*

[15] Park, Jun Michael. "In South Korea Fortune-Telling Will Soon Be a $3.7bn Business." The Economist. The Economist Newspaper, February 24, 2018. https://www.economist.com/asia/2018/02/24/in-south-korea-fortune-telling-will-soon-be-a-37bn-business.

Competitive and Innovative Niche Market within Exposed Culture

By providing alternative responses to modern concerns, diviners build a solid niche market that encourages competition and innovation within a culturally institutionalized environment. This creates external pressures such as family members encouraging and enforcing inexperienced ones to participate in a variety of fortune-telling divination experiences, that thereby stabilizes the balance between supply and demand in the divination market. Because more than 300,000 diviners reportedly reside within an hour of Seoul, there have been numerous divination organizations, institutions, and even an international divination conference.[16] In fact, their overwhelming presence clearly indicates their success in maintaining and expanding their practices. In this segment, I will discuss how the rapid socio-economic modernization first brought religious pluralism, which provided enough room for non-official religions, such as divination, to anchor their presence in religious markets and even serve as a substitute for official religion. Consequently, I introduce three divination valleys, *miari, apkujŏng, and suwŏn* respectively, in and around Seoul metropolitan area to discuss how their communities were able to independently localize, and sometimes jointly with public sectors, to run lucrative businesses in their own distinctive approaches.

Price of Divination Service

In terms of cost, it varies depending on which kind of divination service one prefers nowadays. Starting with the cheapest, tarot would cost 3,000 *won* (roughly $2.75 USD) per question.[17] A typical *saju* (FPD) costs from 50,000 *won* to 10,000 *won*, whereas the individual *mudang* can cost between 50,000 to 300,000 *won* (roughly $35 to $2,700 USD). To a larger extent, *mudang* in Seoul can charge from 3,000,000 *won* upwards to 10,000,000 *won* (roughly $2,500 to $9,000 USD) to sponsor a *kut*.[18]

---

[16] Yoo, "Evolutionary Adaptation," 550

[17] Park, "In South Korea Fortune-Telling,"

[18] Min, Juli. "The Women Who Speak for the Gods." Hazlitt, May 9, 2018. https://hazlitt.net/longreads/women-who-speak gods#:~:text=Shamans%20in%20Seoul%20can%20charge,roughly%20%2435%20to%20%242%2C700%20USD).

Kim, Taemi. Tony Kwon. St. Louis, 3/17/22.

Inherent Religious Pluralism and Polytheistic Rationality

Divination as a pseudoscience serves as a quasi-religion in Korea. Surprisingly, the impact of divination, as a non-official religion, is equally proportional to two dominant official religions - Buddhism and Christianity. According to scholar Andrew Eungi Kim, he states that

> *Nonofficial religion, also called "folk," "common," or "popular" religion, refers to religious and quasi-religious beliefs and practices that are neither accepted nor controlled by official religious groups.*[19]

Because divination has been deeply embedded in Korean culture, people simply take this practice for granted. So, what triggered Korean society to widely accept divination as more than non-official religion?

The driving factor of such an outcome is the structural transition from monotheistic to polytheistic rationality. For instance, after encountering the International Monetary Fund (IMF) financial crisis and globalization, Korean society began to question the shortcoming of monotheistic rationality within existential uncertainty.[20] Thus, a substantial portion of the Korean population suggested that they hold nonofficial religious beliefs in combination with official religious beliefs.[21] In effect, allowing an environment where people can worship more than one God constructed many Koreans, irrespective of their piety, to actively experience various kinds of divination and eventually shape the religious market to be pluralistic in South Korea.

By dint of religiously pluralistic society, the local diviners, as "merchants" within the religious market, opportunely welcomed new patrons who once believed or still believed in the other official religions. Thus, this historically intertwined form of pseudoscience became more widely accepted and eventually could expand into current Korean society. The following sections cover how three divination valleys strategically institutionalize and increase the demand of the divination market in South Korea.

---

[19] Kim, Andrew Eungi. "Nonofficial Religion in South Korea: Prevalence of Fortunetelling and Other Forms of Divination." Review of Religious Research, vol. 46, no. 3, 1 Mar. 2005, pp. 284–302., https://doi.org/10.2307/3512557.

[20] *IBID.*

[21] Yoo, "Evolutionary Adaptation," 562

Geographical Advantage with Isolated Systemization and Creative Competition

According to historical records regarding divination villages, it showed that diviners' residential communities so destroyed such that they were expelled out of the four main gates of old Seoul until the early 1930s. The early diviners had no choice then, so they settled in their new home adjacent to Seoul.[22] Once crowded with prostitutes, refugees, new settlers from rural areas, and other underprivileged groups, the early diviners volunteered to collectively settle in *miari*, now a northern part of Seoul. Fortunately, the diviners' geographical proximity between the village they resided in and the valley they worked in created their own close-knit divination community, as well as a local market. The close-knit atmosphere of the community was heightened by the fact that diviners within the community prevented new outsiders from joining. However, this also had the unintended effect of preventing free-market competition, which ultimately led to the decline of this village. A pedagogical system, however, could have kept the *miari* valley from its eventual decline. This system would allow for the selection and training of a limited number of recruits.[23] Such ways of transmitting knowledge from generation to generation fulfill the demand of divinators in the market, which helps prevent a downturn.

In fact, there are still many divination communities in and around Seoul. Take *apkujŏng* as an example. Considered the heart of Seoul, this divination valley is full of young and financially stable patrons who practice religious freedom. Interestingly, this divination valley evolves to creatively compete with its neighboring churches and temples and even maintain an equal relationship with clients. Being a member of the valley does not entail any religious loyalty. While these two former valleys are known to be Seoul-centric, the following valley is the most successful and promising divination site where local diviners actively engage with municipal government officials to promote their practices.[24]

Cooperation with Municipal Government

With more than 100 individual divination shrines, the Suwon municipal government helped to establish the Suwon divination valley as a cultural tourist attraction. In this valley, divination then became a form of cultural property.[25] As

---

[22] Yoo, "Evolutionary Adaptation," 554

[23] Yoo, "Evolutionary Adaptation," 558

[24] *IBID.*

[25] Yoo, "Evolutionary Adaptation," 557

a result, this divination valley helped Suwon to be commercially recognized as "Divination City". Thus, local diviners are able to innovatively interact with local public sectors to make a suitable divination business model, which has already become a cultural asset in South Korea.

Divination as Nationalism

In the early 1970s, besides the situation in Suwon Valley, the South Korean government utilized the presence of divination in building its national identity. Even though the Korean government initially suppressed and isolated divination, among other folk religions from modernized society, the frequent appearance of divination shifted this mindset to reconsider folk traditions, even that of divination, as a significant part of cultural heritage that needed to be conserved. By doing so, the government heavily played a role in building a reputation for divination communities. For instance, the government appointed some distinguished diviners (both *yŏksulga* and *mudang*) as intangible national treasures and even provided support to many divination communities to help them preserve their ritual practices. Because Korea encountered numerous challenges such as Japanese colonialism (1910-1945), the Korean War (1950-1953), and other kinds of political and economic stagnation during the twentieth century, the promotion of nationalism among the masses or the so-called nation-building process was key in removing this chaos. Thus, divination served as a tool to build nationalism, politically inspiring individuals' active participation in the market and strengthening sovereignty.[26] The three distinctive trajectories of local divination communities and their niche markets demonstrate astute localization, which increases the importance of their presence and persistence throughout Korea.

Family Culture

The divination market would have not flourished without the demand side of the divination market. This section covers how divination was culturally embedded in Korean society, to the point where one is frequently exposed to divination from a young age. In this respect, the demand of this market is often created or maintained by external pressures such as one's own family members. Contrary to how scientific matters operate, pseudoscientific ideas are often communicated

---

[26] Kim, "Nonofficial Religion," 297

through informal sources such as family members, friends, and social media.[27] Despite its colloquial means of communication, the relationships between the divination patrons and their unexperienced loved ones are so intimate that transmission and revitalization of pseudoscience, especially divination, can be easily achieved. Cajoling their relatives and surrounding figures into divination, these patrons are neither evangelizing nor receiving any financial reward. Instead, patrons simply volunteer. So why do people voluntarily let family members join or create their experiences surrounding divination?

The following qualitative studies by scholars *Jiwoong Song, Jieun Chun, and Jiyeon Na* seek to find the correlation between the frequency of divination (FPD) patrons' visit and their degree of trust towards divination (FPD). In their studies, the young participants whose first divination experience happened either as a teenager via their parents or in their twenties by themselves were randomly assigned and their degree of trust towards divination (FPD) was measured within the stage of 1 (being no trust that has a negative consideration towards FPD) to 5 (semi-professional that takes divination matter seriously and even encourages others to participate). The result was quite surprising: the degree of trust had improved (increased) for all participants, regardless of their starting stages, over time as they encountered divination more and more. Under parental control over their decisions, Korean students at a young age were either encouraged or forced to visit shrines with their parents. For instance, the scholar Song et al state

> *Family culture and environment like the presence and influence of mother and grandmother served as the most important factor that led participants to their first experiences. The positive experiences of friends and other surrounding people also played influential roles.*[28]

In fact, what motivates these parents to bring their children to diviners is the overwhelming pressure on the students because of college entrance exam, which happens only once a year. While seeming trivial or something not as important to Westerners, this test evaluates one's academic performance and can end up determining one's entire life. Cultural factors, such as one's family culture that encourages one's children to experience divination out of the parents' will, appeared to be the most influential factors to maintain its prevalence in South

---

[27] Blanco, Fernando, and Helena Matute. "The Illusion of Causality: A Cognitive Bias Underlying Pseudoscience." Pseudoscience The Conspiracy Against Science, January 12, 2018, 45–75. https://doi.org/10.7551/mitpress/10747.003.0007.

[28] Song, Jinwoong, Jieun Chun, and Jiyeon Na. "Why People Trust Something Other than Science." Science & Education 30, no. 6 (2021): 1387–1419. https://doi.org/10.1007/s11191-021-00243-w.

Korea. As academic achievement becomes one of the most common modern concerns, especially among the parents in this peninsula, it is apparent that the size of demand is closely aligned with the popularity of modern concerns. In this aspect, it is understandable why younger generations happen to encounter divination and have a higher chance to improve their degree of trust in it based on their experiences. Ultimately, this is to maintain the richly demanding population of the divination market.

Cognitive Understanding and Acceptability of Pseudoscience

I exclusively covered the historical presence and systematic evolution of divination communities in Korea, but this next segment will closely investigate the mental and emotional strain between patrons and diviners as well as how their communication style epistemically influences patrons' perceptions towards divination. By analyzing the cognitive process of how people accept pseudoscience, I point out how the practical role of pseudoscience as science in the early period inevitably cemented its presence in South Korea.

Motivation behind Divination

Even though the field of concern constantly changes and is constructed over time, there is one common denominator. People's daily happenings are unexpected and vague, especially, when it comes to making major decisions, such as buying houses, marriage, and employment; all decisions that affect someone's life in the long run. With limited time and knowledge, people rarely solve problems to their full satisfaction. Therefore, people tend to lean towards the solution that simplifies their concerns to relieve their stresses and fulfill their curiosity.[29] This is where the divination steps in to serve as a desirable technique for solving patrons' concern to an acceptable degree from generation to generation.

---

[29] Kim, interview.

Why Stubborn Science?

According to Psychology scholars Koslowski and Kuhn, they claimed that

> *The established beliefs are very resistant to change that it is easier to form new belief than its it reviews existing beliefs.*[30][31]

Likewise, the persistence and resilience of these coexisting beliefs of scientific and pseudoscientific ideas are not unusual cases for everyone. Because our intuition cannot always make good judgments, people easily fall into pseudoscience—not because they are intellectually challenged or gullible, but because they cannot trust their own judgments. Sometimes, this intuitive mechanism gets distracted or even malfunctions due to other factors. Perhaps the pseudoscientific practice of divination because it was once considered a practical science, has remained a valid form of science even today. I have coined this 'stubborn science' since no amount of counterproof can dissuade believers of pseudoscience. Humans are predisposed to 'trust' within their epistemic systems; however, other factors often keep this instinctual trust from functioning properly.

Communication Strategy and Patron Relations Management

An ethnographic interview done on Seoul diviners who specialized in *saju* illustrates two different methods of communication employed by diviners. First, establishing a pleasant atmosphere during the divination service boosts the patrons' confidence to actively engage with divination. For instance, the diviner *Haedong-nim* is entertaining and animated during his readings, a style he developed from his previous divination experience.[32] As an experienced diviner, *Haedong-nim* knows how to break the ice and build a comfort zone, where clients can fully depend on him, allowing him to comfortably address their concerns. During his divination service, he believes that divining etiquette should involve maintaining the patron's mental wellbeing. For instance, even if his reading indicates one's tragedy, accident, or even death, is imminent, he keeps the reading to himself.[33] Whether his prediction happens to be right or wrong, his intention of concealing what's portent serves to prevent his client from fear, retaining the pleasant

---

[30] Koslowski, B. (1996). Theory and Evidence: The Development of Scientific Reasoning. Cambridge, MA: MIT Press.

[31] Kuhn, D., Amsel, E., and O'Loughlin, M. (1988). The Develop? In U. Goswami (Ed.), Handbook of childhood cognitive development (2nd ed.), pp.497-523.

[32] Kim, David J. "Four Pillars and Four Diviners," 309.

[33] *IBID.*

atmosphere for the listener. Of course, not all Korean diviners practice in this way. And the power of such an atmosphere should not be ignored. While these diviners provide a hopeful and positive experience, this is not necessarily beneficial to the client in the long term given that the diviner's prediction will happen in the future. So, alternative diviners choose to report bad omens to their clients in a euphemistic way. Instead of directly stating "You will get swindled within the coming month," the desirable response would be "You should be aware that you may lose trust in someone close to you within the coming month"[34] Using this method, even if patrons cannot prevent the destiny told by fortune diviners, patrons become more vigilant and form trust in their fortune. Second, another way for diviners to build credibility is to look more professional. A current diviner, Ms. Kim, is one example. A female *saju* practitioner who lives in Seoul considers herself a life counselor on top of being a diviner. On the back of her business card, written in English is: Human Relations Development Institute.[35] Simply put, by giving one's business card with an embellished title of her occupation (which is a *saju* practitioner), the diviners can appear more reliable to prospective customers. Using such a method, diviners receive higher customer evaluations and benefit from gaining habitues (perpetual clients) or growing their customer base.

Generalized Prediction

An interview with a current diviner, Mr. Chu, corroborates how the technique of using generalized responses to the patrons' concerns makes them become epistemically negligent. As part of the tradition, diviners first retrodict clients' past to gain credibility. In this phase, the diviner Chu often begins with widely applicable statements such as "You had a stressful childhood," to lead the conversation. This works very well in South Korea given the competitive educational system. This open-ended space leads to the next phase of predicting the clients' future.

> *Explaining the particulars of how the future will actually unfold is secondary to giving his patrons what they want to hear, especially in terms of future job prospects and relationships: "You will find happiness, success, and love." The precisions of yes and no, the negative and positive analytics of saju, are transformed into affective sensations. The reading becomes more akin to a "moment of play," or*

---

[34] Kim, interview.

[35] Kim, David J. "Four Pillars and Four Diviners," 319.

even gambling, than prophecy—the moment right before the cards are flipped, or fate is revealed, is what is desired by consumers, and in turn produces more desire. [36]

By generalizing their claims, diviners, like Mr. Chu, cleverly guide their patrons to believe their open-ended predictions. This method puts patrons in an epistemically vulnerable state, meaning that these patrons are more likely to accept whatever incidents that happen to them as something meaningful and correlated to what the diviners predicted. Thus, the way diviners generalize the prediction of one's concern weakens the patron's epistemic vigilance, allowing clients to easily contextualize the diviners' phrases to incidents in their daily lives.

Heuristics

One way to understand the difference between science and pseudoscience, or 'stubborn science', is that pseudoscience seeks confirmation whereas science seeks falsification. [37] Simply put, 'stubborn science' is confirmed through fortune confirming incidents, while science is validated through disproving the former. As previously mentioned, after Yoon Seok Yeol was elected as 20th South Korean president, media and netizens began to question the efficacy of divination practices, such as writing the king sign (王) on one's palm will bring one greater bureaucratic fortune. Because the former candidate, Yoon, has now become president, which 'proved' he achieved greater bureaucratic fortune. This type of reinforcement of divination has recently made the public more accepting of divination. Divination often finds itself reinforced in South Korean society, hence why it has remained so strong in South Korea today.

Overall, it is not unusual that people believe in stubborn science. The interviews of the three diviners show how their communication style strategically set them up to actively engage the patrons in their divination service. With this form, the way diviners leave the open-ended interpretation of the patrons' fortune with generalized claims maintains both the popularity and the stubborn nature of science.

---

[36] Kim, David J. "Four Pillars and Four Diviners," 318.

[37] Stemwedel, Janet D. "Drawing the Line between Science and Pseudo-Science." *Scientific American Blog Network.* Scientific American, October 4, 2011. https://blogs.scientific american.com/doing-good-science/drawing-the-line-between-science-and-pseudo-science/.

Concluding Remarks

In conclusion, divination as a form of pseudoscience has long been integrated into Korean culture. Historically, the divination communities encountered numerous political pressures and socio-cultural movements. However, despite such changes and challenges, these early diviners were better prepared on understanding how divination works and on adjusting the theoretical framework of this spatiotemporally sensitive subject in advance. The main factor that critically influenced the theoretical framework is the societal structure that further extended both the type of concern and the range of patrons. However, the continuing feature throughout history is our desire to know what will happen in the future. To this date, the local diviner's frequent involvement in developing their own market contributed to achieving rich competition, innovation, and even cooperation with the government, which in return, strengthened the nation-building process. However, the divination market would have not been stabilized if not for rapid modernization and globalization that encouraged religious pluralism and a family culture that encouraged one's family to enforce inexperienced ones to try out divination services at a relatively young age. Lastly, the effective communication style and the relationship between diviners and clients provide context to how one can easily become epistemically negligent and eventually fall into pseudoscience. Thus, the resilience of divination in IT giant South Korea would have not been accomplished if the local diviners did not carry out collective achievement, which helps to answer how the presence of pseudoscience is constructed mainly by social, cultural, and cognitive factors. In fact, not all diviners necessarily reject genuine science. Rather, we have come to the stage where both modern science and pseudoscience (divination) are able to coexist and bilaterally interact within society. Therefore, South Korea remains distinct in its culture as it has accomplished and continues to foster the lasting coexistence of science and pseudoscience.

The Remedy for Madness: Treating Mental Illness Throughout Korean History

Chloe Sachs

Abstract

This essay explores the role of mental illness throughout Korean history and the influence of traditional medicine on the development of psychiatric treatment and understanding. Beginning in the Chosŏn dynasty mental illnesses have appeared in personal and medical texts. Early conceptions of mental health depended on Confucian and shamanistic thought and the role of emotions and flow of energy in relation to physical and mental health. The stigma surrounding mental illness has propagated into the modern era, and the Japanese occupation solidified the role of traditional medicine in Korea. Traditional medicine has endured in both helpful and harmful ways, creating a Korean legacy but simultaneously obstructing modern mental health understandings and treatments. The current mental health crisis in Korea is the result of centuries of enduring ideology and the unique identity of Korean medicine.

Introduction

Psychiatric disorders have been treated with varying levels of credibility across cultural and temporal contexts. The lack of physical symptoms and limited brain imaging or viewing technology diminished the credibility of mental illnesses among physicians and societies. Therefore, mental ailments have been subject to various proposed causes and treatments by both healers and philosophers. The Western conceptions of mental illness as a biological disorder with pharmaceutical and therapeutic remedies are now widely accepted in the modern globally-connected world. However, traditional and cultural norms surrounding mental illness persist in modern societies and remain unique to each civilization. As a result, the contemporary diagnosis and treatment of psychiatric illnesses are not merely empirical but also dependent on socio-cultural factors and local history.

Throughout Korean history, folk philosophy and religion defined the general understanding of one's mental state and psychology. The practice of science in the Chosŏn dynasty predated the methodological and empirical nature of experimental sciences, and therefore the study of psychology and medicine lacked systematic experimentation. Buddhism, shamanism, Christianity, and Confucianism created a picture of mental health linked to bodily health. Still, mental illness was often viewed as physical and environmental imbalances rather than a disease that could be cured with medical treatment. Conceptions of medicine shifted as experimentation gained popularity and biological ideas from the West were integrated into medical practice. However, although the societal perception of physical health and disease transformed to align with modern medicine, traditional beliefs surrounding mental illness remained, especially among non-Western educated communities. Korea developed a unique niche for mental illness that combines Korean folk medicine with modern psychiatric theory. Historians have identified exclusively Korean definitions of mental illness such as *hwabyung* or 'fire disease,' The diagnosis of *hwabyung* has persisted since the Chosŏn dynasty and superimposes traditional beliefs onto current diagnoses. I argue that traditional conceptions of mental health treatment developed during the Chosŏn period and were based on theological and ideological notions of the human body rather than empirical science; however, the transplantation of Western biological conceptions of medicine into Korean society resulted in a hybridized traditional and modern understanding of mental health, resulting in stigma and societal resistance against accepting psychiatric diseases as biological illnesses.

Traditional Context

Before Confucian ideology solidified during the Chosŏn dynasty, folk traditions of shamanism and spiritual causes for physical and psychological illness dominated the Korean belief system. Although Confucian ideology entered the Korean court during the Silla dynasty in the 4th century CE,[1] ordinary people still consulted shamans to treat illnesses, especially those of the mind. Shamans treated patients when malevolent spirits took over their bodies and attempted to appease and eliminate spiritual harm to humans within their community. Even during the earliest recorded period of Korean mental illness, peculiar mental functions were treated as problems that had to be exorcized from the body.[2] Koreans viewed symptoms of psychological struggles such as hallucinations and abnormal behavior as so strange they could have no human origins. Blaming the spirit world for mental illness created an inherently negative and shameful correlation. Rather than a disease to treat with pharmacological or therapeutic remedies, shamans believed mental differences to result from an outside influence that could be removed to return people to their "normal" state.[3] The strange and abnormal connotations surrounding mental illness have had lasting consequences on mental treatment in Korea. shamanism depended on the locality and was not homogenous throughout Korea; and subsequently survived in rural regions and as an influencing ideology while medical practices modernized

Korea borrowed and adapted much of its early institutionalized medical theology from China; therefore, Korean medicine acquired and maintained distinct aspects of Confucian ideology. China adopted Confucianism as the state religion soon after its inception. Confucianism emphasizes the link between internal harmony and harmony within the community and mandates rigid constraints about how to live a proper life.[4] Knowledge often traveled southward from China to Korea; however, the movement of ideas was not linear. As medical and miscellaneous information entered Korea, it transformed to fit the new cultural setting of Korea. Confucianism similarly reached the Korean peninsula through the northward

---

[1] Cartwright, Mark. "Confucianism in Ancient Korea," World History Encyclopedia, World History Encyclopedia, 23 Apr. 2022.

[2] Theodore Jun Yoo. It's Madness: The Politics of Mental Health in Colonial Korea. Oakland, California: University of California Press, 2016.

[3] Yoo. It's Madness: The Politics of Mental Health in Colonial Korea.

[4] Cartwright, Mark. "Confucianism in Ancient Korea."

route,[5] and with it came the Chinese structure of institutionalized medicine. However, foreign ideas about medicine must have come in contact with traditional shamanism, and the rigid framework of Confucianism integrated aspects of folk conceptions of mental illness. The *Tongŭi pogam, Treasured Mirror of Eastern Medicine*, written in the early 1600s, was written by a court physician[6] and exhibited the unique development of treatment for psychological illnesses within Korea.

Tongŭi pogam was written by Hŏ Chun, a prominent royal physician during the Chosŏn Dynasty. His writing reflects the Chinese tendency to rely on both pharmacological and uniform medical treatments and a continuing belief in spiritual possession. His writings approach madness as something that could be solved with empiric practices. However, Hŏ Chun still attributes the causes of mania, anxiety, depression, and other illnesses to supernatural imbalances or an irregular composition of the human body. His book provides evidence for the evolution of Chinese medicine within Korea. It took on characteristics of folk beliefs and created a uniquely Korean form of medical and mental health practices.

Hŏ Chun addresses mental disorders multiple times within the comprehensive tome. He first addresses anxiety in Volume I. His analysis of anxiety is situated within the section on emotions. Hŏ Chun connects physical illness to illnesses of the mind and excess of emotion. Anxiety, according to him, is attributed to "qi and vessels [getting] blocked, cannot flow, and they disconnect so they cannot flow up and down."[7] Qi is a concept from Chinese medical philosophy and represents the flow of life's existence throughout the body. Hŏ Chun's characterization of anxiety incorporates accepting Chinese knowledge within Korean medicine. The *Tongŭi pogam* was representative of a unified Korean medical identity and represented the Chinese influence on Korean medicine.

In Volume I, Hŏ Chun also addresses Manic Psychosis, and his treatment recommendations depict the influence of Chinese medicine and Korean folk shamanistic treatments. He attributes Manic Psychosis to "people who get angry

---

[5] *IBID.*

[6] Hŏ Chun, Sangwoo Ahn, Ohmin Kwon, Jeong Hwa Lee, Nam-il Kim, and Wung Seok Cha. *Tongŭi pogam = Treasured Mirror of Eastern Medicine* (Seoul, Korea: Ministry of Health and Welfare, 2013).

[7] Chun, *Tongŭi pogam*, 140.

and become insane."[8] Again, Hŏ Chun pulls from the Chinese source, the *Inner Classic*, and corroborates the Chinese diagnosis. Similarly, physicians attributed mental illness to an excess of emotion, in this case, anger. The royal physician has many herbal recommendations to treat psychosis, including iron, turmeric, and qi Decoction[9]. He discusses many causes of Manic Psychosis and different treatments from distinct sources. Remainders of shamanism also influence some of his treatment options. Hŏ Chun recommends the "Calm Heart Elixir"[10] for when ghosts have possessed an individual. Remnants of folk ideology and the impact of the spirit world upon mental health remained central to Korean understanding. Confucianism did not embrace ideas surrounding the supernatural and spiritual causes of illness. However, in *Tongŭi pogam*, there was still a belief that vengeful ghosts could possess the human body causing physical symptoms. Even within the Chosŏn court and within the most respected levels of medicine, traditional beliefs surrounding mental illness survived.

Similarly, Volume V contains an entire chapter on mania and its various causes. In the introduction, Hŏ Chun states that a cause of mania is if "one's mind is unsound and one is frightened easily, a malicious ghost attacks or haunts the person."[11] He blames spiritual possession on the patient for the weakness of the mind. He even asserts that "there are no actual external pathogens," and that individual's personal failings cause Mania. Therefore, mental illness was blamed on the individual rather than treated as a genuine biological illness. He continues the pattern of stigmatizing psychological illness by treating it as a moral deficiency rather than something out of the individual's control. Most of the treatments are to exorcize spirits, again emphasizing the longevity of shamanistic beliefs.

The Shift to Empirical Medicine

Even as the Chosŏn dynasty transitioned towards Sirhak "practical" learning and empirical experimentation during the 18th century, the legacy of responsibility for mental illness resting on the individual remained. The shame surrounding personal or familial mental illness continued to develop and solidify throughout this period. Sirhak learning was the importation of "modern" intellectual studies,

---

[8] *IBID*, 167.

[9] *IBID*, 169.

[10] *IBID*,167.

[11] *IBID*, 2572.

which situated itself in the Confucian ideology of the Korean state. Rather than demarcating a break from the traditional belief system, it was the intersection between the traditional past and new foreign knowledge. Sirhak medicine reflected this, with aspects that continued from shamanistic and Confucian practices and novel medical ideas that entered Korea through China. Empirical experimentation was a natural development of Sirhak learning. Donald Leslie Baker defines Sirhak as "both a return to the original spirit of ancient Confucianism and as Korea's version of the empiricism, pragmatism, and nationalism that gave birth to the modern West."[12] Sirhak medicine represents the intersection between the revival of past philosophical thought in a new modern context. The medical philosophy of Sirhak was embedded in the Confucian environment of the period and allowed for the acceptance of experimental results, but only when it conformed to traditional thought. It used observation and testing to determine how the world worked but within a strict Confucian framework. Empirical learning had clear implications within the field of medicine. Physicians and ordinary people began to test medical remedies rather than relying on spiritual or energy flow explanations. While experimentation dominated physical health treatment, the prejudices and supernatural beliefs surrounding mental illness remained.

The Encyclopedia of Daily Life: A Woman's Guide to Living in Late Chosŏn Korea, written by Yi Pinghŏgak (1759-1824)[13], exemplifies the empirical nature of medicine during this time while simultaneously displaying the continuation of traditional views surrounding mental illness. Yi was a housewife from a middle-class background, and her encyclopedia gives a unique insight into the regular life and knowledge of women in the Chosŏn dynasty. She writes in detail about many practical and herbal remedies for maladies, specifically female diseases, such as birthing and raising healthy babies. However, Yi's section on "Words for Treating Anxiety" takes on a very different tone. She states, "in the instance of a foolish person this disease is originally not curable."[14] Mental health is again dependent on the personal characteristics of the individual. Yi contends that if one cannot be

---

[12] Baker, Donald Leslie. *Sirhak Medicine: Measles, Smallpox, and Chŏng Tasan,* (University of Hawai'i Press), https://www.jstor.org/stable/23717867.

[13] Lee, Janet Yoon-sun. "The Matrix of Gender, Knowledge, and Writing in the *Kyuhap Ch'ongsŏ.*" *Sungkyun Journal of East Asian Studies* 17, no. 2 (2017): 211-232.

[14] Pettid, Michael J., and Kil Cha. "Volume 4, Pregnancy and First Aid." In The Encyclopedia of Daily Life: A Woman's Guide to Living in Late-Chosŏn Korea (11:136–204. University of Hawai'i Press, 2021), 170.

cured of anxiety, it must be attributed to a personal failing. She published this work for her family's consumption, and it traveled among common women in the Chosŏn dynasty. Her words mirrored the atmosphere in the dynasty concerning psychiatric health and influenced the beliefs within her community. She additionally writes, "the one who does not have illness in their mind is not greedy, and the one who is ill in their mind always seeks carelessly."[15] She correlates mental instability with greed, an inherently negative and self-inflicted characteristic. Therefore, Yi Pinghŏgak spreads the message that psychological disorders are both moral deficiencies and preventable, creating an atmosphere of embarrassment and suppression around mental struggles.

Coexistence of Traditional and Western Psychiatry

A massive shift occurred within Korea when Western psychiatry was introduced during the Japanese occupation. Western psychiatry had already been accepted in Japan due to German influence, and it quickly spread into Korea[16]. Japan hijacked the Korean state medical system during the occupation and reformed it to fit Japanese standards. Medical schools were built in Korea to teach Western-style medicine, mostly for the benefit of Japanese students. Similarly, hospitals to treat psychiatric patients were constructed, where Freudian methodologies and psychiatric therapies became widely used, especially in cosmopolitan areas. The Japanese forged a connection in Korea between neuroscience and spread medical knowledge of the biological causes of mental illness. Ideas of social Darwinism also entered Korea, which emphasized a biological basis for mental illness[17]. Science based understandings of medicine represented a significant shift from traditional concepts of psychological disorders attributed to malicious spirits or lack of emotional self-control. Before this point, Western psychiatry had no real influence in Korea, despite being introduced by Christian missionaries and other academic figures. Traditional medicine won out until the Japanese forced a new psychiatry system onto the Korean academic sphere. Medicine was a colonial arm of the Japanese empire, and by controlling the medical institutions of Korea, the colonial government governed and had access to the lives of individual citizens. The

---

[15] Pettid and Kil Cha, "Volume 4, Pregnancy and First Aid," 171.

[16] Jeong, Haeyoung. Archaeology of Psychotherapy in Korea: A Study of Korean Therapeutic Work and Professional Growth. Routledge, 2018.

[17] Theodore Jun Yoo. *It's Madness : The Politics of Mental Health in Colonial Korea*, (Oakland, California: University of California Press, 2016), 111.

colonial government attempted to destroy Korean agency and unique Korean knowledge; however, it survived, and I would argue it thrived in the face of attempted elimination of the Korean identity.

The continuity of traditional Korean medicine is traceable even into the colonial period when Korea was under Japanese jurisdiction. Korea did not passively receive modern knowledge and technology from Japan. Rather than suppress uniquely Korean medical ideology, Japanese colonization fostered resistance against their oppressors and led to the revival of a uniquely Korean medical identity. This was the development of Hanbang medicine and the renaissance of traditional medical philosophy. In his paper "Hanbang Healing for the World," James Flowers makes a powerful argument about the influence of traditional Korean medical knowledge and the unique renaissance of Eastern medicine in Korea [18]. Hanbang medicine differed from Western medicine because it incorporated aspects of spiritual healing and individual treatment. These were remnants of shamanistic and Confucian healing methodologies, and in consequence, the Hangbang Renessaince represented the revival of traditional medicine. It is unclear whether the return to historical belief systems would have occurred without Japanese occupation. At least, the strong sentiment and enduring adherence to medical tradition is a product of resistance to the Japanese occupation.

The revival of Hanbang occurred with much popularity at the elite level, but among everyday people, it merely prevented Western ideas of medicine from reaching their daily lives. Although the Hanbang revolution depicted a shift in state policy and elite academia, as Flowers argues, there was no danger of the dissolution of traditional Korean medicine in rural and local communities. He writes, "for the majority of Korean people, Eastern medicine had neither disappeared nor been in any real danger of extinction."[19] Traditional Korean conceptions of medicine survived as political and scientific evolution occurred, and the colonial period was no exception. The entrance of Western medicine did not influence common people, and even elites returned to folk medicine when given a choice between modern and traditional medical systems. South Korea has the highest percentage of traditional medicine practitioners in East Asia.[20] I would

---

[18] James Flowers, *Hanbang* Healing for the World: The Eastern Medicine Renaissance in 1930s Japan-ruled Korea, *Social History of Medicine*, Volume 34, Issue 2, May 2021.

[19] Flowers, "*Hanbang* Healing for the World," 9.

[20] Kumar, Hemant et al. "Traditional Korean East Asian medicines and herbal formulations for cognitive impairment," *Molecules (Basel, Switzerland)* vol. 18,12 14670-93. 26 Nov. 2013.

argue that cultural resistance against the Japanese played a significant contributing role in the reverberations of Hanbang medicine into modern Korea. Korea has continued to practice traditional medicine, and it has maintained a dependence on folk medical techniques more so than any other East Asian nation. This proves the longevity of Korean traditional medicine and its ability to persist even in the face of advancing technology. Korea had the opportunity to homogenize its medical system to conform with the rest of the globe, but the academic community actively chose to persist with traditional beliefs.

As mentioned briefly at the beginning of this paper, an example of the longevity of traditional Korean mental health understandings can be seen through *hwabyung* or "fire-illness," which is a uniquely Korean psychological ailment that has survived across centuries and is still used today. Patients diagnosed with *hwabyung* present a range of modern-defined symptoms such as anxiety, depression, obsessive-compulsive disorder, and anorexia nervosa.[21] However, it does not fit into any Western categorization of mental illness. The first reference to *hwabyung* is from court records during the Chosŏn dynasty in 1603. The definition of this illness has survived and is part of the Western and clinically accepted DSM encyclopedia of mental illness classifications. The disease is proof of the longevity of Korean medical knowledge and traditional beliefs surrounding mental illness. A Korean psychiatrist Min Sung-kil reports that "It is problematic that our country's psychiatrists rely solely on theories of Western medicine in treating our country's patients. Socio-cultural factors that cause our patients' mental illnesses are different from those of (Western) societies."[22] Min recognized *hwabyung* as a "culture-bound syndrome" unique to the Korean identity. He argues that Western "advanced" psychiatric treatments are not the most effective for an exclusively Korean illness. He promotes traditional remedies as more effective and shows that Korean psychiatry continued to depend on folk medicine even in the face of Western knowledge. Mental health treatment followed the same pattern as traditional Korean medicine and has maintained many of its historical elements.

Hwabyung is attributed to a blocked qi from the build-up of excess emotion and a subsequent rise of "fire-heat." A psychiatrist, Kim Jung-woo, states that "once the liver loses its distinctive function to regulate the activities of qi, because of excess anger and frustration, the constraint of liver-qi tends to occur. If the liver-qi is

---

[21] Suh, Soyoung. "Stories to be told: Korean doctors between hwa-byung (fire-illness) and depression, 1970-2011," *Culture, medicine and psychiatry* vol. 37,1 (2013).

[22] Suh, "Stories to be told: Korean doctors between hwa-byung (fire-illness) and depression, 1970-2011."

blocked, then the qi probably transforms into heat-fire, thereby leading to an upward counter flow that resembles the symptoms of hwa-byung" (Soyung). Kim's commentary contains many parallels to the *Tongŭi pogam*. He argues that *hwabyung* is caused by the qi blockage, harking back to the Confucian ideology of earlier centuries. Additionally, Kim blames this mental illness on the patients' excess anger and frustration. He continues the historical pattern of blaming psychological disorders on the moral failings and emotional lack of control of the individual. Despite global recognition through the DSM for *hwabyung*, it did not take on the typical characteristics of Western mental illness diagnoses. The disease maintained its Koreaness by relying on Eastern medical explanations for its source rather than pathogenic or neurologic agents.

Additionally, *hwabyung* represents the intersection between traditional Korean and modern Western treatment types. Psychiatrists maintain that counseling is a helpful method for treating *hwabyung*, proving that Western psychiatric beliefs have permeated Korean society to a certain extent. However, Min also states that "It is problematic that our country's psychiatrists rely solely on theories of Western medicine in treating our country's patients. Socio-cultural factors that cause our patients' mental illnesses are different from those of (Western) societies". He maintains that Korean culture is unique and requires specific traditional treatments utilizing Hanbang methods. The renaissance of Hanbang healing did not dissipate with the end of the Japanese occupation, and the revival of traditional medicine impacted conceptions of disease into the modern era.

Modern Implications

Although the continuation of traditional medicine was a positive mechanism for preserving Korean identity and distinctive Korean medicine, it has led to negative repercussions on mental health. Modern-day South Korea has the highest rate of suicide among OECD, Organization for Economic Cooperation and Development, a group of advanced and internationally connected nations[23]. The OECD works to combat social, economic, and political concerns and inequity, one of these being mental health crises. Shared fiscal reliance and knowledge exchange create a degree of standardization among these nations. However, Korea's rate of suicide is 24.6 per 100,000 persons, significantly higher than any other nation in the OECD. Modern-day Korea is accepted as a highly

---

[23] "Health Status - Suicide Rates - OECD Data." *TheOECD.*

industrialized and scientifically advanced nation. Western medicine has been implemented and advanced in most cosmopolitan areas, and Korean scientists have contributed vast swaths of knowledge to the global medicinal network. However, despite industrialization and acceptance of biological causes for disease, mental health treatments are less effective and widely implemented than in other nations.

A reason for this is the continuation of Confucianism and ideas concerning filial piety. Filial piety is a central tenet of the Confucian belief system, and the philosophy has continued in Korean culture and societal norms the waning of Confucianism with modernization. It is defined as devotion to family members, especially elders, to maintain a peaceful society. It holds the obligation to one's family to the utmost value, even before personal happiness and responsibility,[24] and influences much of historical and modern Korean society. A study completed by Soontae An reports, "suicide is regarded as a personal deviance that neglects the responsibility of caring for family members or friends."[25] This study shows that suicide is viewed by society as a failure to uphold the ideals of filial piety and therefore carries an immense stigma. In Korea, suicide is not treated as an uncontrollable symptom of mental illness but is viewed as a sin and a personal deficiency. This likely contributes to the high suicide rates in the country. The article argues that the stigma surrounding thoughts of leaving one's family for "selfish" reasons prevents individuals from disclosing suicidal thoughts and seeking treatment. Rather than discouraging suicide, filial piety expectations prevent those in need of help from procuring it. Confucian remnants of mental health ideas have led to modern-day drawbacks in Korean psychiatric tolerance.

In addition, shame is conferred upon individuals struggling with mental health in South Korea due to the traditional culturally accepted causes of mental illness. As seen from Chosŏn sources such as the *Tongŭi pogam*, causes of mental illness included moral insufficiencies and overindulgence in emotion, and spiritual and supernatural possession due to similar personal flaws. The idea of individual responsibility for mental illness has led to a stigma surrounding mental health that prevents open discussion in social settings. The study by An and others concludes that, "because self-improvement and growth require overcoming negative emotions and hardships in collectivist cultures, East Asian societies value

---

[24] Britannica, T. Editors of Encyclopaedia. "xiao." *Encyclopedia Britannica*, July 1, 2019. https://www.britannica.com/topic/xiao-Confucianism.

[25] An, Soontae, "Social Stigma of Suicide in South Korea: A Cultural Perspective." *Death Studies*, 2022, 1–9.

minimizing, tolerating or suppressing difficult emotions."[26] The value system in Korea has withstood time, and the modern mental health atmosphere reflects centuries-old ideas surrounding psychological disorders. The high levels of stigma are based on the Confucian ideals of society over the individual, emotion being the cause for psychological struggles and controllable. Although Western thought acknowledging that most mental disorders are biological and out of the individual's control is available in Korea, new education has not been provided to the general population and implemented in the psychiatric system. However, the lack of discussion surrounding mental health and the continuation of traditional ideology has had a profoundly negative impact.

Although there are many productive and valuable reasons for retaining traditional Korean medical philosophy, many historical beliefs surrounding psychology and psychiatry are outdated and do more harm than good. Accepted causes for mental illness in Korea must change to meet modern biological standards to improve treatment and lower suicide rates. Filial piety prevents individuals from seeking adequate suicide prevention treatment and promotes stigma rather than preventing suicide. Shame is not an effective inhibitor of mental illness, and in many cases, it seems to make psychological diseases worse. Instead, efforts to address the mental health crisis in Korea need to start at a cultural-societal level and tackle the long-established stigma surrounding mental health.

Conclusion

Ultimately, the repeated instances of integration of traditional ideology into modern intellectual thought and the renaissance of traditional knowledge incited by resistance against the oppressive Japanese state led to the continuation of historical mental health stigma and cultural refusal to accept Western psychiatry and the normalization of psychiatric health. Shamanism and Confucianism are immutable within Korean medicine and have survived and prospered since the Chosŏn dynasty. From these early philosophies, mental illness has been construed as individual weakness. This idea persisted in modern-day psychiatry after the revitalization of Korean medicine in retaliation against Japanese colonization. *Hwabyung* provides evidence for traditional Korean medicine's unique and enduring characteristics and the constructive impacts of identifying the cultural components of mental illness. However, in general, traditional medicine has been

---

[26]*IBID.*

a drawback in mental health treatment and the societal understanding of mental illness and generated a strong stigma preventing individuals from seeking treatment. A balance must be struck between maintaining Korean identity in medicine and dispelling the stigma that has provoked a mental health crisis.

Old and New Collision: Preference for Traditional Korean Medicine

Ashley Lee

Abstract

There is little question that the colonial period was pivotal in the development and spread of modern Western medicine in Korea. Did this, however, serve as a trigger for traditional Korean medicine's general decline? While previous research has primarily focused on the concept of Uisaeng (traditional Korean medicine doctor) and medical policies implemented by the Japanese Government, this paper begins with the Korean herbal medicine industry and investigates the distribution and consumption of Korean herbal medicines during the colonial period from three perspectives: the policies for Korean merchants by the Japanese government, the changes in the Korean herbal medicine industry, and the consumption of Korean herbal medicines in the Korean society. This paper demonstrates that, during the colonial period, when old and new ideas collided, most Koreans preferred traditional Korean medicine, including upper-class elites and intellectuals who were open-minded about emerging concepts and options and had ample opportunities to receive western medical treatment. The Korean herbal medicine sector, one of the pillars providing medical assistance to the public, changed appropriately while depending on its own tradition's inertia. The vigor and dynamism of the sector during the colonial period highlight the need to correct the one-sided narrative of medical modernization in relation to Western medicine.

Introduction

When Shilhak intellectuals studied western medical science in Chinese books, it was introduced to Joseon. Korean envoys paid a visit to Italian missionary Matteo Ricci's Catholic church in Beijing. The introduction of western medical knowledge to Korea was made possible by these envoys who brought foreign materials translated into Chinese.

Many scholars were fascinated by the anatomy and physiological functioning of the human body as described in western medical publications. Looking into the human body was deemed "savage" in the Confucian culture in which they lived, and even investigators who solved murder cases were not allowed to dissect the victims[1]. In Jeong's Inoculation and Comprehensive Treatise on Smallpox, another Shilhak scholar, Jeong, Yak-yong, wrote on the theory of smallpox inoculation. In his book Discourses on the Body and the Soul, Hanki Choi contrasted Western and Eastern medical sciences. Furthermore, there is evidence that certain Catholic Shilhak scholars were given smallpox vaccinations, but Western medical expertise remained theoretical and confined to Shilhak intellectuals. After signing the Treaty of Ganghwa with Japan, Joseon opened its doors to the world in 1876 where standardized practical medical procedures were established. Previously, the Joseon dynasty had a rigorous policy against introducing new ideas and customs. Because the king was too young to reign, Ha Eung Lee who was the father of the Gojong and the king of Joseon at the time, ruled in his place. Lee was apprehensive about having cultural contacts with other nations, although Gojong was open to it. When Gojong declared himself ruler of the kingdom and forced his father to resign, Japan saw an opportunity and pushed Joseon to open. Since then, industrial items, philosophy, and a number of other Western ideas and materials have flooded Korea. Among them was Western medical science.

---

[1] People who believed in Confucianism thought that a dead body should be buried unharmed.

Korean Medical Science Under Government General of Korea (GGK)

Through the Regulation of Uisaeng, published in 1913, the Government-General set tight limits on the issuing of Uisaeng licenses, expiration dates, and sites of practice. On the other hand, it established a more permissive management strategy toward merchants, with the primary idea of separating dispensation from prescription. The Government-General enacted and issued the "Pharmaceuticals and Pharmaceutical Business Ban" in 1912, following Japanese legislation (1887). Pharmacists (dispensing medicines based on physicians' prescriptions), drug vendors (selling medications), drug manufacturers (producing and selling pharmaceuticals), and patent medicine sellers were all classed as relevant pharmaceutical practitioners under the decree. Simultaneously, in July 1913, the colonial authorities released "Regulations for Pharmaceutical Inspection," which regulated the medication business. The aforementioned decrees, however, could not be applied to the Korean herbal medicine sector, regardless of the division of associated practitioners or the aims of drug management, because they were founded on Western medical norms.

As a result, the Government-General issued a series of administrative measures to control merchants from June 1912 to July 1916, referring to them as individuals who sell Korean herbal remedies in a certain province only after acquiring a license from provincial governors. Traditional Korean medical practitioners were divided into two categories: Uisaengs and merchants. In addition, the colonial authorities established a functional split of medicine distribution powers between physicians and pharmacists, stating that Uisaengs may only give herbal medicine to their own patients, whereas merchants could dispense only by prescription. However, when it came to selling a specific herbal remedy, such sales were completely unrestricted since, with the exception of a few very poisonous substances, "herbal medicines differed from their western equivalents and were not governed by pharmacopoeia."[2]

Because the merchants were not Uisaengs and were not considered medical experts, obtaining a license to sell medicinal plants was easier than obtaining a Uisaeng license. Initially, merchants could receive a permission by filling out an

---

[2] "Document on the Preparation of Drugs by Korean Medicine Merchants," Gyeongmuhwibo 124, July 1916, p. 131.

application, but in 1923, an exam system was implemented.[3] Despite its introduction, exam results were not the primary criterion for granting the permission until the 1930s, and questions were based on traditional herbal knowledge. As a result, the merchants' certification test was easier than that of the Uisaengs or Western medicine apothecaries. Unlike the Uisaeng license, the permission was perpetual. Furthermore, in terms of nationality, both Japanese and Koreans worked in Western medicine apothecaries, although Koreans were the only ones who worked as medicine merchants. In comparison to other businesses, Koreans dominated the Korean herbal medicine industry and the medicine merchant became more approachable and desirable to Korean culture at the time.

Unlike the steady drop in the number of Uisaengs from 5,800 in 1914 to 3,300 in 1944, the merchants' population grew from over 7,000 in 1914 to over 10,000 in the early 1920s.[4] Although the population steadily decreased after then, it remained over 7,000 until the end of the colonial period. In the overall medical sector, merchants made up the biggest proportion of practitioners. Western medical practitioners, like as pharmacists and apothecaries, rapidly rose during the colonial era, but by 1942, their number had plateaued at 2,000, less than one-third of the merchants. Even the combined number of Uisaengs and Uisas (Western medicine physicians) was less than the merchants. At the same time, unlike Western medical physicians, chemists, and apothecaries concentrated in Kyungsung and other cities, merchants had a large representation in each town. With the exception of a tiny number of Chinese merchants, all other merchants were Koreans. Therefore, they had a natural affinity for Korean culture. Because there were few doctors in certain rural regions, the merchants' position became even more important.

Uisaengs are traditional Korean medicine practitioners with a license, and some of the merchants with outstanding medical abilities are traditional Korean medicine practitioners who sell Korean herbal medication. This mirrored the fact that the distinction between Uisaengs and merchants was not always obvious at medical locations, owing to the difficulties of obtaining an Uisaeng license. Many people who aspired to be doctors changed their minds and became merchants, while merchants changed their minds and became Uisaengs. Like the Uisaengs,

---

[3] Shiroishi, 1918: 106; "The Drugstore Also Has a Test System, If You Fail the Exam, You Cannot Even Run a Pharmacy," Dong-a ilbo, April 15, 1923.

[4] Huang Yong-yuan, Traditional Korean Medicine Doctors and the Colonial Modernity of Traditional Korean Medicine during the Japanese Colonial Period, Ph.D. diss. (Korea University. 2018).

many merchants at the period not only sold Korean herbal remedies but also evaluated the patient's pulse and suggested therapy.[56] Those who obtained the Uisaeng license, on the other hand, ran Korean herbal stores while also treating patients.[7] This revealed that Korean herbal stores were a crucial medium for the survival of traditional Korean medicine throughout the colonial period, as well as a vital to increasing the use of Korean herbal remedies.

Unlike the Uisaengs, merchants had less constraints throughout the colonial period and maintained a significant presence. This, however, was not the colonial authorities' intended action—like the Uisaengs, the Government-General had allowed the merchants' presence after considering Korean medical customs and the lack of personnel to administer Western medicines. The colonial authorities, who intended to wait for the popularization of Western medicine and the phasing out of traditional Korean medicine, believed that the merchants would be replaced as the number of pharmacists increased. Because the nature of the business of the Uisaengs and merchants was linked, with the former issuing prescriptions and the latter delivering medication, as the number of Uisaengs fell, the number of affiliated merchants decreased as well[8]. In other words, the colonial authorities' imposition of limitations on the Uisaengs while keeping a reasonably forgiving attitude toward the merchants was just a temporary arrangement, not a preference for the latter. The policy's loophole provided a large gap for merchants to exist, allowing them to scrape out a living, if not a fortune, by depending on the massive demand for Korean herbal medicine.

Globalization of the Korean Herb Medicine Industry

The Korean herbal medicine business did not shrink throughout the colonial period, but instead flourished consistently in the face of the progressive popularization of Western medicine and government prohibitions on the growth of traditional Korean medicine. Aside from the existing medical need, the industry's growth can also be linked to merchants' reactions to the situation—they

---

5 "An Introduction to New Kimpo: the Authority of Korean Herbal Medicine—Yun Byeongcho, the Owner of Ilsim-dang Herbal Store," Dong-a ilbo, December 8, 1937.

6 "A Medical Master: Yeongheung-dang Pharmacy Gang I-seong," Dong-a ilbo, October 30, 1934.

7 Yun Byeongcho, New Kimpo, 1937.

8 Gang Hyeok, "My Humble Opinion about Oriental Medicine Revitalization Policy at the Time of Its Publication," Oriental Medicine, July 1, 1939, p. 28

played a key role in the circulation and commercialization of Korean herbal medicine. Imported medications and Korean domestic drugs circulated in the Korean market at the period; all would either enter the market through merchants or be accessible at local Korean medical clinics or hospitals, purchased through herbal medicine marketplaces in Daegu, Jeonju, Daejeon, and other cities. In any case, merchants were the primary source of Korean herbal medicine distribution and commerce, as well as the primary link between market and customer. As a result, during the colonial period, their efforts essentially controlled the market's course.

Some merchants continued to sell traditional decoctions and pharmaceuticals while concurrently making and selling patent medicines after getting a sales authorization from the authorities, considering Korean medical traditions and society's requirements. They were quick to adjust to shifting circumstances. As a result, traditional Korean herbal medicine has embraced its variety and has begun to commercialize and sell. The Korean herbal medicine industry may be split into three groups based on different foci of the core business, market aims, the owner's self-recognition, and public image: traditional, mixed, and ginseng-exclusive. The following section gives an overview of the many types of Korean herbal stores and their features.

Types of Korean Herbal Stores

Traditional drugstores supplied Korean herbal remedies such as dry medications, decoctions, traditional tablets, ginseng, and velvet deer horn solely or predominantly. Despite the fact that a variety of Western pharmaceuticals had reached the Korean market by that time, demand for herbal treatments remained strong. "Koreans have taken herbal medicine since ancient times," Kim Hak-chun, the proprietor of Gongan-dang Drug Store in Anseong's Gyeonggido market, remarked in 1927. "Although a lot of Western medicines have entered Korea presently, the sale of herbal medicine continues to increase steadily."[9] As a result, many Korean herbal stores continued to operate as usual, and some even grew to be large.

Contrary to traditional herbal medicine stores, which continued to sell traditional herbal medicine, mixed type stores not only supplied general Korean herbal remedies but also actively pursued patent medication development and sales. The

---

[9] "Biographies of Successful Businessmen (31): From a Drugstore Servant to a Korean Herbal Medicine Giant," Dong-a ilbo, February 12, 1927.

traditional medicine market began to shift after the entry of Western medicine and Japanese medication vendors following the port's opening. Some merchants reacted positively to the changed scenario and sought for new opportunities, such as joining the patent medication industry. They used Western pharmaceutical techniques to create patent medications in addition to traditional Korean tablets, plasters, and powders. In comparison to traditional decoctions, individuals found it much simpler to consume patent medications.[10] It also assisted the marketing of herbal medicine and helped herbal retailers increase their earnings.

One of the most distinguishing features of the Korean herbal medicine business was the use of Korean medicinal herbs as the primary raw material in the manufacturing and distribution of patent medications. The commercialization of Korean herbal shops was facilitated by the creation and selling of patent medicines utilizing Korean medicinal herbs as raw materials. This subsequently aided their transformation from traditional to contemporary pharmacies, and even pharmaceutical corporations. Faced with fierce competition in the patent medicine market, major Korean herbal stores embraced modern marketing and management techniques such as trademark registration, advertising, promotion, remittance settlement, and the establishment of branches and agents, all of which helped to accelerate the transformation of the traditional Korean herbal medicine industry.[11]

Exclusive ginseng shops were the third type of Korean medicinal store. Unlike other therapeutic plants, the advantages of Korean ginseng were identified early on, and it became well-known in both East Asia and western nations such as the United States. In addition, because ginseng was extensively utilized as a complementary medicine in East Asia, there was a high demand for the substance. As a result, not only did common herbal stores offer it, but a set of chambers of commerce devoted solely to the plant arose. Of fact, because the colonial government imposed a strict red ginseng monopoly, folk ginseng sellers were limited to only dealing in white ginseng[12].

The globalization of the drug market was a crucial characteristic of the traditional Korean herbal medicine industry's commercialization. During the colonial period,

---

[10] Yang Jeong-pil, Commercial Traditions and Capital Accumulation of Modern Gaesong Merchants, Ph.D. diss. (Yonsei University. 2012).

[11] Suh Soyoung, Naming the Local: Medicine, Language and Identity in Korea since the Fifteenth Century (Cambridge & London: Harvard University Press, 2017).

[12] "The Sacred Herb of the World, a Study on Korean Ginseng," Dong-a ilbo, May 15, 1934.

the industry operated in a global atmosphere and developed internationally. First, there was a brisk trade in Chinese medical herbs (Tangjae, as opposed to Chojae, a Korean medicinal plant). While the Korean herbal medicine community employed nationalist slogans like 'non-dualism' to underline that local medicinal plants were preferable than Chinese ones after the liberation, the latter were essential inside the community during the colonial period. Furthermore, during the colonial period, Korean emigration soared. However, because they were unable to modify their lifestyle and felt that seeing a doctor in an unfamiliar country would be cumbersome, abroad Koreans continued to rely heavily on Korean herbal stores and physicians. As a result, the Korean herbal medicine sector has spread internationally (Jung, 2014). Koreans ran a lot of medicinal stores in Japan and Northeast China, some of which were quite substantial.

Context of Old and New Perspectives

Although traditional Korean medicine and Western medicine coexist in modern Korea, the general people, particularly young Koreans, appear to feel that the former is losing favor. The roots of this occurrence are not examined in this work, but it is suggested that these changes may have impeded young scholars from making an impartial assessment of medical care throughout the colonial period. According to existing research, the Korean community, particularly in rural regions, was not covered by the Western medical system throughout the colonial time. Instead, it was shunned from the "field" that contemporary Western medicine embraced. Traditional Korean medicine was impacted by colonial authority throughout the colonial period, yet it remained one of the most essential ways for Koreans to preserve their health[13]. The emphasis of traditional Korean medicine, Korean herbal remedies, were therefore important to the common Korean.

On the other hand, citizens just wanted to choose between different medical treatments to find a cure and prevent illnesses. People at one medical practice were making selections on various therapies based on distinct circumstances rather than sticking to a predefined treatment method. Such a choice highlighted the colonial period's intertwining and exchange of old and new ideas in the medical

---

[13] Lee Geod-me, A Study on the General Public Understanding and Utilization of Korean Traditional Medicine in the Colonial Period, Korean Journal of Medical History 15-2 (2006).

sector, as well as their active reaction to sickness. It symbolized the period's struggle between tradition and modernity.

To begin, we must admit that Koreans' attitudes toward Western medicine steadily changed from fear and hatred to acceptance and approval in the 1910s. They thought that taking Western drugs was suicidal, and that Western physicians were death agents. However, within a few years, this dread and unfamiliarity had dissipated dramatically. For example, on May 12, 1916, Maeil sinbo reported,

"Western and Korean medicine have begun to co-exist. Everyone can seek medical treatment in accordance with their preferences. People who admire Western medicine opt for that treatment, including general medicine and surgery; similarly, people who value Korean medicine receive Korean medical treatment; people who decide on medical treatment according to their situations usually choose Korean remedies for general medicine and western cure for surgery. This is not an absolute choice and there are various views"[14].

However, it was clear that people were overcoming their distrust of Western medications, and medical treatment preferences appeared to be more diversified.

This did not, however, imply that the two systems were at odds. First, as previously said, Western medicine physicians and pharmacists were concentrated in metropolitan regions at the time, severely limiting access to Western treatment. Second, most Koreans could not afford Western drugs due to their high cost. Patients would often attempt patent medications, Korean herbal remedies, or other folk cures first, and then then seek aid from Western medical experts if everything else failed[15]. They were turned away from hospitals even if they went there because of their socioeconomic position. The high expense of Western medications and therapy, as well as the issue of money worship, have thus been important themes of discussion since the 1920s. This fact was brought to light in the preceding scenario. Poor people, according to Western medicine specialist Seo Young-hwan, only deserve Korean medical therapy. The choice between Korean and Western medicine seemed to be inextricably linked to fortune and social prestige, establishing a new barometer of social standing.

However, it was not just due to financial restraints that Koreans preferred to seek Korean herbal medication. The evolution of Western medicine during the colonial period should not be overstated. In reality, many ailments could not be

---

14 "Ever-changing Medicine and Traditional Korean Medicine," Maeil sinbo, May 12, 1916.

15 "The New Women. Let's Destroy Superstitions," Dong-a ilbo, March 23, 1927.

cured with Western medicine at the time. In the fall of 1918, for example, the Spanish flu struck Korea, infecting 7.5 million people out of a population of 17 million. 0.82% of the population died[16]. While Western doctors were useless, the Uisaengs' traditional Korean remedies, such as Toxin-Vanquishing Powder, Harmonious Flow Decoction, Flesh-Resolving Decoction, and Ephedra Decoction, yielded positive outcomes. The aforementioned Korean medications were allegedly used by Japanese settlers and Western medicine practitioners alike.

Furthermore, to ease the effects of the Great Depression on the Korean countryside, the Government-General began the Campaign of Award for Cultivating Medicinal Herbs across the nation in 1933. The public at the time referred to it as "the golden era of medicinal herbs" and "the heyday of Korean herbal medicine," leading many to assume that the situation had changed again after many years of the expansion of Western medicine to the East[17]. As the Sino-Japanese War began in 1937, the import of not just Western medications but also Tangjae from China reduced substantially, increasing Korean society's reliance on Korean-made herbal treatments. We can conclude with certainty that Korean herbal medicine was neither neglected or severely influenced by the arrival of Western medicine throughout the colonial period.

On a micro-level, the diary of this person is investigated in order to provide a picture of the consumption and medical condition in Korean society. There was a man named Lee Byeong-gon who was an expert in medicine and followed the Confucian physician's tradition. As a Confucian intellectual, he was interested in whether he might utilize his medical skills to treat his parents' illnesses as a gesture of respect. Medical supplies in the isolated countryside were scarce, thus learning more about medicine was a battle for life. He had a collection of traditional Korean medical texts that he used as a source of medical information. Furthermore, Lee Byeong-gon's cousin, Lee Byeong-won, established a Korean herbal store, which assisted his family in accessing medical care while also promoting his medical skills through communication.

In Lee Byeong-gon's journal (1906–1945), we learn that when he or his family became ill, he frequently sought treatment at Kim Hwa-sun, Kim Dong-su, and

---

[16] Kim Taek-jong, The 1918 Influenza Pandemic and Japanese Government-General of Korea's Preventive Measures against Epidemics, Seoul National University, Journal of Humanities 74-1 (2017)

[17] "With the Advent of the Korean Herbal Medicine Era, Scholars also Went on a Trip to Look for Famous Drugs, as Did Kei-jo Imperial University," Dong-a ilbo, February 19, 1933

Kim Jong-chae's herbal store, which was approximately 2 kilometers away. If the medication didn't work, he'd drive another 8 kilometers to Milyang-eup, or even further, in quest of help. When his mother became ill on May 8, 1911, he went to Kim Hwa-herbal sun's store for the first time. After his mother did not respond to them, he traveled to Daegu, more than 60 kilometers away, on May 13 to invite Jang Du-hwan to cure her, but he was unable to see the doctor. Lee thereafter invited Kim Hyeon-chan to Changwon-gun, a 50-kilometer drive away, twice. He had also asked Lee Chun-hae to visit him in Busan, which is 80 kilometers away, for diagnosis and prescriptions for himself and his family, as well as seeing physicians in Busan. He had a lot of options for medical therapy[18].

Lee Byeong-gon, as previously said, was unprejudiced toward modern western civilization and hence did not reject Western medicine. However, there were few records on Lee and his family's treatment with Western medicine, aside from the fact that they occasionally took so-called "Japanese medicine" (possibly patent medicine) and that he visited a Japanese hospital in Milyang-eup for issues like face ringworm, tooth filling, and foot disease in 1929 and 1931. Lee Byeong-gon clearly cannot be compared to a senior figure like Kim Yun-sik in Kyungsung in terms of medical resource availability. However, given Lee's financial capacity to fund extensive trips to cities like Daegu, Changwon, and Busan, as well as bringing traditional medicine physicians to his home, it is reasonable to assume that his family could readily acquire Western medical care if they so wished.

Certainly, Lee Byeong-gon does not represent Koreans throughout the colonial period. However, his experience reflects the picture of medical practices in colonial Korean culture, in which old and modern remedies worked together. Unlike the impoverished masses who could only afford Western medicine, Lee Byeong-gon benefited from better geological and economic conditions, as well as greater access to Western medicine. Nonetheless, he continued to use Korean herbal medicines as part of his regular treatment—Western medicine was only a supplement or an alternative. One explanation for this, is tradition's rigidity, in addition to the fact that Western medications were not always helpful for disorders that could not be healed by traditional Korean treatments. Western medicine lacked wider appeal and was unable to break traditional Korean medicine's hegemony in the medical sector.

---

[18] Toesujaeilgi (National Institute of Korean History, 2007).; Korean J Med Hist 2020; 29(1): 215-274.

Conclusion

The colonial period was a critical moment for Western medicine to establish root and spread in Korea in terms of decrees, systematic techniques, public health, medical education, hospitals, and medical practitioners. If we merely look at it from the standpoint of the Uisaeng, it is indisputable that traditional Korean medicine experienced a significant crisis as a result of colonial laws restricting the Uisaengs in numerous areas such as legal status, licensing, and education. However, if we study Korean herbal medicine and examine the historical scenario from the standpoint of medical consumption, we must evaluate the following: is our perception of contemporary medical care in the colony influenced by the reality of the modern Korean medical industry? Eastern and Western medicine did not undergo a dramatic alternation in colonial Korea, whether in the medical sector or in the daily lives of ordinary people, and the latter did not significantly impact Korean society's medication consumption pattern. Western medicine became more or less an alternative for individuals in both cities and villages—for the most part, it was just a complement to Korean medicine in their routine medical care. This is true even for those in the middle and upper classes who did not suffer financial or geographical barriers to accessing western medical care. The foregoing research explains why the Korean herbal medicine sector remained unaffected during the colonial period. If the above facts are true, we must reposition traditional Korean medicine in medical history and the narrative of medical modernization during the colonial period, and pay more attention to traditional Korean medicine's inheritance and change, as well as the interaction between Eastern and Western medicine.

Marketing Ginseng: Empire, Export, and the Establishment of Korean Identity

Leah Ford

Abstract

Ginseng has been critical in Korea since its introduction to the peninsula, dating back to the early 6th century A.D. The herb has become an indispensable plant when it comes to medicinal treatments in traditional and contemporary Korea. After the end of the Chosŏn dynasty (1392–1910), the Korean peninsula had to open its doors and accept new ideas and ways of life from nations other than China. During the colonial period, ginseng became an exportable commodity under the framework created by the Japanese colonial system. Prior to this period, ginseng was considered a regional resource, the Government-General of Korea (GGK) legitimized ginseng as a worldwide export and unintentionally made the herb a symbol of Korean unified identity. This created the foundation for the modern market that Korea is still capitalizing on. While legitimizing ginseng, the GGK started to push against the Korean use of traditional oriental medicine in favor of Western medicine, but the usage of ginseng persevered despite medical evidence that challenges its supposed efficacy. Now, ginseng is still a staple in everyday Korean homes because of its historical, medicinal, and national monetary value.

Introduction

Why does South Korea hold nearly half of the world's ginseng revenue? As Michael Kim explains,

> *producers appropriated Japan's imperial science to give legitimacy to their products. Therefore, when assessing ginseng's colonial legacies, we must consider not just the role of the colonial state, but also the role of private producers that pioneered new consumer markets.[1]*

By taking a deeper look at the colonial period and analyzing the consumer markets, we will see a transition in the perception of ginseng compared to the perception during the Chosŏn era because of the role of private companies. James Flowers adds to this discussion by analyzing some private companies' creative but successful marketing tactics when promoting ginseng.[2] During the late Chosŏn Dynasty, ginseng was considered a regional resource. When Japan annexed Korea in 1910, the Government-General of Korea (GGK) created a ginseng monopoly that legitimized ginseng as a worldwide export and later unintentionally made the herb a symbol of unified Korean identity. This monopoly created the foundation for the modern market, which Korea is still capitalizing on. This paper establishes the historical context of Korean ginseng and explains how the herb was perceived in China, Japan, and Korea. Finally, the paper addresses the reasons and effects of the GGK monopoly on the herb, which will explain the foundation of the modern ginseng market.

Ginseng as Regional Resource in the late Chosŏn

Ginseng has always been an essential herb in the Korean peninsula, but the year 1613 marks a watershed for Chosŏn herbal medicine. This was the year renowned royal physician, Hŏ Chun (許浚, 1539–1615), published *Tongŭi pogam* (東醫寶鑑). The book's purpose was to compile all existing medical knowledge in China and Korea, but Hŏ Chun went beyond that by "giving more detailed accounts of the

---

[1] Michael Kim. "The Pitfalls of Monopoly Production and the Ginseng Derivatives Market in Colonial Korea, 1910–1945." *Seoul Journal of Korean Studies* 30, no. 1 (2017): 3-30. doi:10.1353/seo.2017.0001.

[2] James Flowers, "Koreans Building a New World: Eastern Medicine Renaissance in the Context of Japanese Rule, 1910-1945" (dissertation, 2019), pp. 1-390.

names and qualities of local botanicals than had ever appeared before."[3] The book included different preventive medical techniques that ordinary people could follow. One treatment even tells readers how they can use ginseng to "rescue the lungs."[4] Due to valuable information found in the book,

> *There was high demand for Tongŭi pogam from China and Japan, and they searched desperately for copies of Tongŭi pogam. When envoys from China visited Korea, they invariably asked to obtain copies of Tongŭi pogam. Because it was published in Japan first, Japanese doctors were able to make full use of Tongŭi pogam before Chinese doctors were. But after China came to appreciate its value, it was published in China more than 30 times.*[5]

Despite being published about 400 years ago, the book is popular amongst traditional oriental doctors today, as it is still considered the "'bible' of Oriental medicine" since it accelerated the use and development of folk medicine.[6]

A few years after *Tongŭi pogam* was published, tensions arose on the Sino-Korean border because of ginseng, which was known for its "medical efficacy, mysterious age, rarity, and physical features."[7] French priest Pierre Jartoux (1680–1720), was able to test out the medical efficacy for himself when " he accompanied an imperial tour to Manchuria, reported on the antifatigue properties of ginseng as a sovereign remedy for all weakness occasioned by excessive fatigues either of body or mind," which shows that the knowledge of its benefits were not limited to East Asia.[8] The Chinese knew about the miraculous powers held by the herb, so they, too, sought ginseng. By crossing the border into China, Korean merchants traded

---

[3] Soyoung Suh,"*Hŏ Chun's (1539–1615) Tongŭi pogam (Precious Mirror of Eastern Medicine)." In Chinese Medicine and Healing: An Illustrated History*, edited by TJ Hinrichs and Linda L. Barnes, 137–139. Cambridge MA: Harvard University Press, 2013.

[4] "English Translation of the Donguibogam." Korea Institute of Oriental Medicine. Accessed April 22, 2022.
https://kiom.re.kr/modedg/contentsView.do?ucont_id=CTX001017&menu_nix=jFB45u4H&srch_mu_lang=ENG.

[5] "Donguibogam: the Korean Traditional Medicine Book." National Library of Korea. Accessed April 13, 2022. https://www.nl.go.kr/EN/contents/EN30701000000.do.

[6] Sungchul Kim, Bong-Keun Song, and Jin-Hee Won. "Historical Medical Value of Donguibogam." *Journal of Pharmacopuncture* 19, no. 1 (March 2016): 16–20. https://doi.org/10.3831/kpi.2016.19.002.

[7] Seonmin Kim. "From Frontier to Borderland." *In Ginseng and Borderland: Territorial Boundaries and Political Relations Between Qing China and Choson Korea, 1636-1912*, 1st ed., pp 19–46. University of California Press, 2017. http://www.jstor.org/stable/10.1525/j.ctt1w8h1p0.9.

[8] *IBID.*

and sold ginseng to the Chinese in exchange for payments, titles, and sometimes gifts. While different dynasties did buy Korean ginseng, the Qing dynasty blamed the Koreans for damaging the ginseng market and hurting their sales.[9] They insisted that Koreans be jailed for trespassing on Chinese lands to poach ginseng. The Qing dynasty "considered ginseng not only a special resource growing in Jurchen territory but also a symbol of the Jurchens themselves" and not the Koreans.[10] They believed non-Jurchens should not be able to handle ginseng, which led to a Qing dynasty monopoly on ginseng. While the Ming courts were eager to receive the best ginseng from Korea and, "considered ginseng a unique local product of Korea," the Qing dynasty did not. They delegitimized Korean ginseng by calling the herb a "local product of the Manchus" and stopped accepting ginseng as a tribute from the Chosŏn dynasty.[11]

Ginseng was well known amongst everyone during the Chosŏn dynasty, from the poorest farmer to the richest king within the Korean peninsula. It was especially favored by King Yŏngjo (1694–1776), who

> *was famous for taking ginseng for a long time, and the amount he took between the ages of 59 and 73 exceeded 100 kŭn (60,000 grams) King Yŏngjo loved ginseng so much that he took approximately 20 kŭn (12,000 grams) in a single year when he was 72 years old.[12]*

Even though there were disagreements between him and his physicians about his intake, Yŏngjo was the longest living king of Chosŏn. As an elder, he consumed more than 40 kg (88 pounds) of ginseng as a restorative medicine. The popularity of ginseng was also noticeable to everyday people. While the cost of ginseng remained the same throughout King Yŏngjo's reign, this exact cost began to be expensive to everyday people. Yu Man-ju, a commoner, wrote in his diary in 1778, "…ginseng is the number one treasure in this nation, in this century. Generally right now, (the) usage of ginseng is very extreme, and its cost is very high." [13] Man-Ju also noted the way medicine was approached was beginning to change. People began turning away from drugs "such as rhei rhizome (rhubarb) and natrii sulfas

---

[9] *IBID.*

[10] *IBID.*

[11] *IBID.*

[12] Seong-su Kim. "From Woohwang Cheongsimwon (牛黃淸心元)* to Ginseng (人蔘) - the History of Medicine Use in the Joseon Era -**." Korean Journal of Medical History 26, no. 2: pp 147–80. Accessed April 26, 2022. https://doi.org/10.13081/kjmh.2017.26.147.

[13] *IBID.*

(glauber's salt), to restorative herbal medicine, such as ginseng and cervi parvum cornu (dried deer velvet)."[14] Shortly after the end of King Yŏngjo's reign the cost of ginseng soared as the demand increased. Ginseng merchants started to search for new production centers.

During the eighteenth century, Japan's desire for Korean ginseng started to grow. Although other forms of ginseng existed, Japan specifically sought after *hongsam* (red ginseng) because it was said to be more potent than the other variants: "ginseng was by far the most important of the several dozen varieties of drugs imported to Tokugawa Japan from Korea."[15] According to Sŏngho Yi Ik, a philosopher, and scholar, "the Japanese considered ginseng a powerful medicine and were willing to fight and die to buy it. Thanks to this belief in its potency among those of neighboring countries, ginseng was treated as an important gift in international diplomacy."[16] Unlike in Korea, the main issue for the bakufu's ("Japanese government") was that ginseng could not be grown on Japanese lands. After spending so much money importing ginseng from Korea, high-ranking officials requested that they figure out a way to grow ginseng locally. Of the ginseng grown locally, the people were not satisfied with herb. This defeat led to multiple trips to Korea to find the perfect ginseng seed that could be grown in Japan and have the same taste, appearance, and other features that would be identical to their neighboring country. They even began to get help from Korean scholars to grow the perfect ginseng plant that would be cultivated across Japan. During this period of practicing local production, Japan imported ginseng seeds, but cultivation failed to reach a sustainable level during the first half of the seventeenth century. After decades of continuously trying to reach successful cultivation, Japan eventually triumphed. In 1746, Japanese "herbalists, medicine merchants, and bakufu officials had sought to learn all they could about ginseng, through visiting Chinese doctors and merchants in Nagasaki, and other Korean doctors who visited Japan."[17] Once Korea became an imperial colony, Japan seized the opportunity to make ginseng one of their most valuable exports. Korean ginseng was a prize to be captured.

---

[14] *IBID.*

[15] Daniel Trambaiolo. "Diplomatic Brush Talks and Medical Journeys: Eighteenth- Century Dialogues between Korean and Japanese Medicine." Studies in History and Philosophy of Science, 2013, pp 93–113. https://doi.org/10.1007/978-94-007-7383-7_6.

[16] "Ginseng." National Institute of Korean History. Accessed April 25, 2022. http://contents.history.go.kr/front/eng/tz/view.do?levelId=tz_b31.

[17] Trambaiolo, "Diplomatic Brush Talks," 102

Ginseng, Export, and Korean Identity in the Colonial period (1910–1945)

Ginseng consumption was common during the Chosŏn period, but once 1910 arrived, and Japan annexed Korea, it was expected that the usage of ginseng in medicine would soon be a thing of the past as Japan desired to modernize Korea, now a colony of its empire. This modernization emphasized Western medicine in direct contrast to the traditional Korean medical system. This opposition created the unity behind Korean identity. Because Western medicinal professionals were the only ones licensed, it alienated Koreans from traditional Korean sources of medicine. The GGK tried to push traditional medicine out of Korea as far as possible. However, despite their best attempts, there was still a local market of Koreans looking for traditional medicine. The colonial authorities downgraded traditional medicine doctors and did not allow these doctors to be given honorary titles. The government's plan to eliminate traditional medicine ultimately failed since "the shortage of Western medical personnel was too great to care for the whole population," which is why traditional medicine could survive.[18] These traditional doctors were only recognized to cope with the lack of Western medical doctors. Nevertheless, to meet the shortage of available Korean medical personnel trained in biomedicine, the GGK licensed a category of practitioners trained in Sino-classical medical traditions that became loosely categorized by various terms such as *hanbang* (Chinese medicine; J. *kanpō*), *tongŭi* (Easterm medicine), and *Chosŏnŭi* (Korean medicine).[19]

Even though these professionals were given licenses to practice, "they did not have government public facilities therefore research and practical techniques could not be developed."[20] By the end of the colonial period, about 70% of the doctors were western medicine doctors. Unexpectedly, the decrease in traditional doctors did not decrease ginseng usage at home. Meanwhile, the GGK saw great monetary value in the herb.

The monetary benefits of ginseng were no longer supposed to be amongst the Koreans, but they were meant to be enjoyed by the new government. At first, the

---

[18] Seung-pyo Hong, "Traditional Korean Medicine in the Modernization Process: Institutional and Attitudinal Changes" (dissertation, 1989), pp. 1-166, https://dr.lib.iastate.edu/entities/publication/7badfa14-d99a-4b37-b82e-f9dc52ed0e93.

[19] Sonja Kim, "From the Ŭinyŏ to the Yŏ'ŭi: The Female Physician." In *Imperatives of Care: Women and Medicine in Colonial Korea*, pp 51–77. Honolulu: University of Hawaii Press, 2019.

[20] Hong, "Traditional Korean Medicine," 64

financial benefits of ginseng came from tactics such as those used by GGK memebr Sudō Hisaemon (須藤久左 衛門). In 1916 he spent one-year researching ginseng, then went to Seoul and started the business, Chosŏn cheyak hapcha hoesa (朝鮮製藥合資會社), which was considered the representative of a successful ginseng extract company. The company was so successful that he returned to Japan to establish an office in Tokyo and create lucrative ginseng markets in Taiwan and Manchuria. Because of his company's creative and frequent marketing tactics in the vernacular newspapers, "Sudō's company not only developed the colonial Korean consumer market, for it also distributed its products throughout the Japanese empire," which set the foundation for other Korean ginseng companies that would rise later .[21] The ability to promote ginseng as a health and fitness aid came from the increasing Japanese biomedical research budget. This prompted,

> *Different private companies (to) built different drugstores, such as traditional herbal stores mainly selling traditional Korean medicines, hybrid drugstores that simultaneously dealt with the manufacture and sale of patent medicines, and ginseng drugstores that specialized in the ginseng business. This classification promoted the commercialization of traditional Korean herbal medicine.[22]*

Through this research, companies could promote their ginseng derivatives - soaps, wines, teas, and pills - with Japanese nationalistic themes that directly supported Japanese patriotism. If it were not for the added Japanese patriotism, these products would have gotten taken off the market because they would not have promoted the new leaders.

Around 1920, the GGK ginseng advertisements were usually a brand mark without any text to support the ad. On occasion, the GGK created heavy text advertisements explaining ginseng's health benefits. Private Japanese companies like *Chosŏn cheyak hapcha hoesa* combined traditional themes with modern rhetoric to market ginseng to Koreans. Instead of getting rid of traditional medicine completely, Japanese companies decided to take a vernacular approach and capitalize on Korean spending power. Some of these tactics included promoting

---

[21] Kim, "Ginseng Derivatives Market," 22

[22] Yong-yuan Huang, "'Medicine of the Grassroots': Korean Herbal Medicine Industry and Consumption During the Japanese Colonial Period," *Korean Journal of Medical History* 29, no. 1 (2020): 215-274, https://doi.org/10.13081/kjmh.2020.29.215.

health and fitness beside the health benefits of ginseng in vernacular newspapers because "health and fitness were an integral part of cultural nationalist aspirations for building a strong nation." [23] Around 1910, there were also ginseng advertisements in Korean-published medical journals whose audience was much different from a standard vernacular newspaper, "with urban-educated Koreans as the most likely target audience of advertising in the Eastern-medicine journals, marketing the iconic strengthening herb of ginseng fits the broader political concept of strengthening bodies to invigorate the nation."[24]

Other Korean companies started to develop their own marketing tactics like mail to order services. Compared to the GGK ads, private companies put more effort into their ads by focusing on an audience of people interested in health and fitness and designing their ads to target just that by adding text to give readers more information about the health benefits they would be interested in. These were Japanese ads found in Korean language newspapers that "contributed to the formation of a large market for patent medicines and health supplements among colonial consumers."[25] Scholar Jin-Kyung Park elaborated on the effect of the vernacular advertisements:

> *Thousands of medical advertisements by Japanese pharmaceutical companies emerged at the juncture of imperialism, colonialism, and the expanding transnational medical market. These advertisements did more than sell the products. By serving as visual icons of imperial medical prowess and scientific modernity, and by personifying the preachers of newly available biomedical knowledge and taxonomies of disease to Korean consumers, these ads deeply infiltrated colonial daily life via vernacular newspapers. Arguably, the striking presence of patent medicine ads from Japanese pharmaceutical companies was deeply connected with the ways in which the colonial pharmaceutical business paid close attention to the policies and ideologies of the colonial state and historical conditions within which they had to operate as well as strategically utilize them for their own purposes.[26]*

---

[23] Kim, "Ginseng Derivatives Market," 21

[24] Flowers, "Korean New World," 115

[25] Kim, "Ginseng Derivatives Market," 21

[26] Jin-kyung Park, "Managing 'dis-ease': Print Media, Medical Images, and Patent Medicine Advertisements in Colonial Korea," *International Journal of Cultural Studies* 21, no. 4 (January 13, 2017): 420-439, https://doi.org/10.1177/1367877916687882.

Flowers, like Park, also mentioned the importance of visual icons since "strengthening the nation was not only a metaphor visualized in the form of ginseng and other medicinal products, but also manifested in the organization that was necessary to secure advertising."[27] By tapping into the needs and context of the Korean consumer, the private corporations could directly pinpoint and target their needs. Noting the extensive formation of these new untapped markets due to the ad's success, Japanese and Korean businessmen began to stake their claim in the ginseng market.

The GGK started stating in their ads that they used hongsam as their source of ginseng. This was done to increase the value of the brand since hongsam was known to be expensive.[28] On the other hand, during the latter half of the colonial period, one private company's ginseng tea advertisement "emphasized that their products could serve as a coffee replacement during a period when everyone had to follow the "national policy" (國策) and preserve their "national health" (國民保健)."[29] Even though the monopoly created a significant barrier for Korean ginseng producers, the stark differences between the two marketing approaches show how easy it was for private companies to one-up the GGK and establish themselves in the ginseng market. As mentioned by Jin-Kyung Park, these ads did more than sell the products. While the advertisements were a crucial part of the success of the private corporations, they also had to deal with some controversy. For example, during the 1940s, multiple ads claimed to have ginseng as one of their main ingredients. This turned out to be false and led to the arrest of over ten individuals that were making kangjangje 強壯劑, or "health tonics," which were extremely popular amongst the Korean bourgeois. They added the ingredients to labels so their products could be viewed as a health medication,[30] which shows how much of an impact ingredients like ginseng had on consumers during the colonial period.

By 1920, the GGK began to make efforts to gain even more profit off of Korean ginseng. "They imposed a state monopoly (October 1910 in Korea's)[31] most

---

[27] Flowers, "Korean New World," 115

[28] Kim, "Ginseng Derivatives Market," 21- 27

[29] *IBID.*

[30] *IBID.*

[31] Daily Consular and Trade Reports. United States: Department of Commerce and Labor, Bureau of Manufactures, 1913.

profitable ginseng product, *hongsam*, or "red gingseng."[32] The state monopoly on *hongsam* would later prove to be a bad financial move on behalf of the GGK. "Ginseng (*hongsam*) was produced under the leadership of the government very strictly, and could not be manufactured and sold privately."[33] In addition to the strict monopoly, the GGK gradually raised the ginseng manufacturing facilities scale.[34] This state monopoly did not work in favor of the colonial leaders. In theory, the strict monopoly and increasing scale would have exponentially grown the ginseng revenue, but, that was not the case. The GGK relied too much on China to purchase the majority of their *hongsam*, which did not allow room for other nations to purchase *hongsam* from the GGK because the prices were too high; therefore, the *hongsam* "only appealed to a select group of Chinese consumers who had the spending capacity" which limited the sales the GGK would have received if the prices were more affordable.[35] The total revenue of ginseng went from about 12% in 1921 to about 4% ten years later because of the strict monopoly the GGK imposed on the ginseng market. In addition to the high prices, due to the Chinese boycott foreign products in 1925 and the increasing anti-Japanese sentiment following the Manchurian Incident in 1931, the sales of *hongsam* plummeted. While "Chinese consumers associated "Koryŏ ginseng" with Korea, they were also aware that (the Japanese conglomerate) Mitsui (三井) was its distributor."[36] The Japanese were the cause of the Manchurian Incident of 1931 where,

> *Japanese soldiers blew up a section of the South Manchurian Railway near Mukden (now Shenyang) and began the military campaign which placed all of Manchuria under Japanese control, and the following year, declared its 'independence' from China.[37]*

In retaliation, the Chinese began a nationwide boycott of Japanese goods including ginseng. "These public spectacles of mass foreign boycott campaigns

---

[32] Kim, "Ginseng Derivatives Market," 3

[33] Sang Myung Lee, Bong-Seok Bae, Hee-Weon Park, Nam-Geun Ahn, Byung-Gu Cho, Yong-Lae Cho, Yi-Seong Kwak, "Characterization of Korean Red Ginseng (Panax Ginseng Meyer): History, Preparation Method, and Chemical Composition," *Journal of Ginseng Research* 39, no. 4 (October 2015): 384-391, https://doi.org/10.1016/j.jgr.2015.04.009.

[34] *IBID.*

[35] Kim, "Ginseng Derivatives Market," 13

[36] Kim, "Ginseng Derivatives Market," 12

[37] Sandra Wilson, "The Manchurian Crisis and Moderate Japanese Intellectuals: The Japan Council of the Institute of Pacific Relations," *Modern Asian Studies* 26, no. 3 (1992): 507-544, https://doi.org/10.1017/s0026749x00009896.

simultaneously helped develop Chinese nationalism and *hongsam* exports throughout much of the colonial period."[38] The drastic decrease in *hongsam* sales was a direct result of two factors: the price of *hongsam* being too high for other consumers, which created the dependency on China's purchasing power, and the lack of creating stable political relationships with China.

Outside of the Chinese boycott of foreign goods, there were also other problems with the monopoly, "there were entire categories of ginseng products outside of the monopoly system where the colonial state competed with both Korean and Japanese private producers."[39] Koreans knew the value of their ginseng. If they could get around the GGK monopoly on *hongsam*, they knew they would be able to profit from ginseng as they were during in the Chosŏn period. Kaesŏng ginseng producers were known for their involvement in trade with the Chinese courts during the Chosŏn period and for "developing the *hongsam* production techniques in the eighteenth century (that would) offset the increasing scarcity of wild ginseng," which later set up the area to be known as a high *hongsam* production region.[40] With that in mind, the GGK had a stronghold over *hongsam* production in the Kaesŏng region. The monopoly was not hard to get around if one were able to establish a private company as "the government controlled the *hongsam* centers in Kaesŏng and left the production of *paeksam* in other areas mostly unregulated."[41] The lack of control over *paeksam* led to a rise in private Korean and Japanese ginseng corporations. The decrease in *hongsam* revenue also fueled the increase in *paeksam* or "white ginseng" productions amongst private companies. The GGK also turned to the *paeksam* cultivators when they acknowledged the lack of revenue in the *hongsam* industry. They were to rely on *paeksam* to combat the monetary pitfalls with *hongsam*. It also helped that *paeksam* production was not highly taxed by the GGK, which allowed more Korean ginseng growing regions to increase their *paeksam* productions. There was only a monopoly on *hongsam* because it "had great value as an export item to China (while *paeksam*) had strong consumer demand primarily in Korea and Japan."[42] The people of Kaesŏng started to take matters into their own hands when they realized the *hongsam* profits were no longer as high as they once were. They began to feel the repercussions of the GGKs ginseng monopoly. To combat the effect, they could only privately handle *paeksam*

---

[38] Kim, "Ginseng Derivatives Market," 6-18

[39] *IBID.*

[40] *IBID.*

[41] *IBID.*

[42] *IBID.*

because of the monopoly, and the private *paeksam* corporations began to rise. According to the scholar Michael Kim:

> *The Kaesŏng producers aggressively produced and marketed paeksam in Korea and Japan and China, because they had no choice but to develop other outlets due to the state monopoly on hongsam. Koreans in general had an awareness that ginseng could be one of Korea's most representative products in the world market. An article published in May 1928 in the journal Pyŏlgŏn'gon proclaims:*

> *If we boast of Korea's special products, there are indeed many. But due to time and space limitations, we cannot discuss them all. Without further ado, let us proudly introduce ginseng, the most representative among Korea's special products.*

The recognition of ginseng's export value-led numerous Kaesŏng companies like the *Koryŏ samŏpsa* 高麗蔘業社 and the *Kaesŏng inseam sanghoe* 開城人蔘商會 to use modern marketing techniques such as advertising promotions and mail order services to develop the *paeksam* market.[43]

Despite their efforts to take over the *paeksam* industry, revenue numbers still were not rising as high as the Kaesŏng producers wanted. The producers in Kaesŏng asked the GGK to release their hold on *hongsam* because more profit could be made with *hongsam* than *paeksam*. The Kaesŏng producers became the biggest beneficiary of *paeksam* sales. As the private companies started to make more money, they expanded their business to other Korean herbs.

While the GGK had a more aggressive approach when it came to profiting from *hongsam*, private companies could take their time with the marketing campaigns and dominate the *paeksam* market that the GGK failed to look into. Because the GGK was so assured with their business model on their *hongsam* monopoly, they did not bother with the same type of advertisements that the private companies were creating for their *paeksam* marketing campaigns. Since the GGK would not give up its monopoly, private producers could successfully discover ginseng consumer markets in multiple ginseng derivative categories. The Japanese ginseng consumer market readily purchased derivatives from private companies, and in return, the private companies would link their products to scientific research-based in Japan. While the GGK's dependency on China negatively affected their *hongsam* revenue, private companies could successfully capitalize on Japanese-

---

[43] *Ibid.*

backed research and the Japanese advertising frameworks to promote ginseng and its derivatives amongst non-Chinese consumers. Against the colonial leaders' preference for Western medicine, the Korean herbal medicine industry became one of the few Korean-dominated industries to become successful. The success came from the GGK implementation of Western doctors over traditional doctors. The government did not establish a healthy relationship with Chinese consumers, and they would not let go of their ginseng monopoly. The GGK failed to eradicate traditional medicine doctors in favor of the Western alternative because they did not adequately train a substantial number of doctors to take the place of the traditional doctors. Since they could not create a healthy relationship with Chinese consumers, noticing the negative financial impact, private Japanese and Korean companies took matters into their own hands. They began establishing their customers in the *paeksam* industry.

Conclusion

By the end of the colonial period, Korean ginseng became an everyday cultural commodity for the Koreans when the previous ginseng was viewed as a regional commodity. As eloquently explained by Dr. Flowers, "Korean ginseng became a recognizable everyday commodity. Koreans, from the bottom-up, made use of the imperial networks to promote a "Korean" product."[44]

The transition from regional to local was possible because of the GGK's involvement in *hongsam* production during the colonial era. They imposed a ginseng monopoly only on *hongsam* because they acknowledged the value of the herb the neighboring nation, China. The GGK also thought the monopoly would take ginseng revenue to the "projected bright prospects."[45] The monopoly was used to increase the prices of *hongsam* that would have taken advantage of the Chinese consumer purchasing power. By having too much reliance on one nation and only worrying about gaining money through *hongsam* exports, they failed to realize the large local market in Korea and Japan, which, like the Chinese, had a decent amount of purchasing power when it came to a different type of ginseng, *paeksam*. Private Korean companies suffering from the economic effects of the monopoly were able to effectively follow the marketing guide established by successful private Japanese *paeksam* companies. The marketing guide consisted of

---

[44] Flowers, "Korean New World," 236

[45] "Daily Consular and Trade Reports," 614.

tapping into the interest of the Korean people mainly via Korean vernacular newspapers and mail to order services. These ads were filled with text backed by research centers in Japan and proved how effective the *paeksam* would be for consumers' health. As a result of the success the private Korean companies had with ginseng during the colonial period, contemporary Korea is still reaping the benefits, with numbers reaching around $1.14 billion in 2013 for ginseng revenue for South Korea alone.[46] Ginseng has also become the subject of recent medical research, potentially restoring the lungs[47] and helping cognitive or motor functions.[48]

---

[46] In-Ho Baeg, Seung-Ho So, "The World Ginseng Market and the Ginseng (Korea)," *Journal of Ginseng Research* 37, no. 1 (January 15, 2013): 1-7, https://doi.org/10.5142/jgr.2013.37.1.

[47] Ju Hee Lee et al., "Ginsenosides from Korean Red Ginseng Ameliorate Lung Inflammatory Responses: Inhibition of the MAPKS/NF-KB/c-Fos Pathways," *Journal of Ginseng Research* 42, no. 4 (2018): pp. 476-484, https://doi.org/10.1016/j.jgr.2017.05.005.

[48] Key-Chung Park et al., "Cognition Enhancing Effect of Panax Ginseng in Korean Volunteers with Mild Cognitive Impairment: A Randomized, Double-Blind, Placebo-Controlled Clinical Trial," *Translational and Clinical Pharmacology* 27, no. 3 (2019): pp. 92-97, https://doi.org/10.12793/tcp.2019.27.3.92.

Illuminating Technology and Social Change: Electrical Evolution in Korea

Yael Shaw

Abstract

This research paper traces the distinctive evolution of electricity in Korea from the colonial era to modern day. I set out to provide a broad global context for electricity, as well as dissect the social, economic, and political factors that played a vital role in its introduction and implementation into Korean society. By analyzing existing scholarly works, I not only highlight significant innovations in the field of electricity in Korea, but I also identify their socio-cultural impact on Korean society over time. To do so, I first situate the electrification of Korea on a global timeline. Then, I consult existing texts to examine specific electrical devices and their functional relationship with Korea throughout history. In my analysis, I show how electrical technology has played a vital role in contributing to a growing sense of patriotism, individuality, and national identity in Korea. Finally, I evaluate how electrical innovation has defined social progress and modernization in Korea, arguing that culture in Korea develops around the acquisition and implementation of new electrical technologies.

Introduction

Historians have long grappled with understanding Korea's process of modernization. Yet, very little has actually been explored in Korean literature concerning the true physical and operative transformation of Korea's metropolises and the daily lives of people functioning within them. The study of Korea's electrical evolution subsequently offers a unique window of opportunity to better understand the important factors that drive socio-cultural development towards modernization on a national scale. In particular, what makes electricity in Korea such a great vehicle for exploring societal progress is in part due to its wide multiplicity of forms and uses. By acknowledging this variety of material practices of electrical technology in Korea, including how electrical innovations were first developed and used by practitioners, it is clear to see electrical technologies' subsequent cultural impact on society. As I approach the subject of social progress in Korea through the lens of electricity, I ultimately demonstrate in what ways electrical technologies have not only been implemented to reflect the needs of society, but also, and perhaps most importantly, why and how culture in Korea has developed around existing electrical technologies.

American industrialist Henry Ford is quoted saying:

> *Reading a machine means determining what the artifact says about the people who designed it, the process of its design, the assumptions made about its purposes, the expectations held of its putative users, and the ways it could actually be used.*[1]

This remains true for the study of technologies in Korea; while observing electronic devices in Korea over time, for example, it is imperative that historians of technology take note of both the physical characteristics of the electronic artifacts as well as the social contexts in which they were constructed and eventually utilized. This consequently provides a better, more holistic understanding of Korean society by peeking into the lives of the actual scientific craftsmen who created electrical devices in addition to electricity's daily users. Through this detailed examination, it becomes apparent that such electrical systems, and innovation more broadly, are built by technologists to solve problems and/or fulfill goals in the daily lives of their consumers. This theory is typically

---

[1] Hyungsub Choi, "The Social Construction of Imported Technologies: Reflections on the Social History of Technology in Modern Korea," Technology and Culture 58, 4 (2017): 907.

not contested. I argue, however, that the importation and implementation of electricity in Korea, while perhaps fulfilling a societal need, simultaneously created a socio-cultural revolution that did not simply fit into a pre-existing environment, but rather reconstructed it.

Electricity in Global Perspective

China

The methodical process of harnessing and developing electricity is one of the largest driving technological factors behind modern capitalism and industrialization on a global scale. Near the end of the nineteenth century, as Western countries became armed with imperialist ideas of racial and cultural superiority, the spread of foreign technological penetration accelerated across East Asia. The transfer and assimilation of advanced Western electrical technologies is therefore not unique to just Korea, yet even the differences in modernization patterns across East Asia vary drastically. China's early encounters with Western technology had dramatic rippling effects on traditional Chinese culture. In his journal article review of Erik Baark's piece, "Lightning Wires: The Telegraph and China's Technological Modernization, 1860-1890," Graeme Lang sheds light specifically on telegraph technology in China during the late nineteenth century and its subsequent foreign impact on Chinese territory. In so doing, he provides a detailed examination of the initial resistance to and eventual adoption of the telegraph from the perspectives of both *yangwu* modernizers and *qingyi* traditionalists.

There is a common false narrative that all modern Western technologies were initially desperately sought after and hence immediately welcomed into foreign ports. While electricity eventually served a valuable purpose in global commerce, diplomacy, and daily life, China did not always greet new technologies with welcome arms. Although some modernizers like Li Hongzhang desired peaceful relations with strong Western powers, urging others to accept Western technological influences, other Chinese traditionalists very much "saw in modern technology the instruments of foreign aggression and a subversion of the Chinese political order and cultural values."[2] The telegraph is no exception; despite its

---

[2] Graeme Lang, "Lightning Wires: The Telegraph and China's Technological Modernization, 1860-1890 by Erik Baark," *China Review International* (1998): 353.

beneficial properties, it took years for Western imperialists to successfully convince Chinese authorities to introduce and implement the new technology into China. In large part due to the military incursion by Japan into Taiwan in the 1870s— when Qing officials found that the telegraph actually allowed foreigners in Beijing to know more about the daily progresses on the edges of the empire than even the empire's own ministers—Chinese sovereignty over Taiwan became a prime consideration for allowing a short telegraph line construction to finally occur.[3] Later, with little overt opposition from locals, a second line was planned between Fuzhou and Xiamen.[4] Although the line seemed mutually beneficial to both the Great Northern Telegraph Company and the provincial government at first, disagreements among officials eventually led to construction sabotage, and the line was never built.[5] Despite the Fujian-Xiamen line failure, the telegraph did eventually become widely accepted and enforced by Chinese authorities throughout the 1870s. By 1880, Chinese officials built government-controlled telegraph lines and even opened schools to train Chinese staff on telegraph function and utility. It is now difficult to imagine a world before the telegraph, but important to acknowledge its slow introduction to the Chinese nation and the dramatic social, economic, and political factors that restructured daily life during the Qing dynasty.

Japan

Considerably more literary work has been published on Japanese history during this period of electrical influence than on both China and Korea combined. That is not surprising; during the age of Western imperialism, Japan was a model modernizer that markedly paved the way for the development of East Asian industrialization as a whole. Around the time of the Meiji Restoration, a political revolution in the late 1860s that overturned Japan's feudal system of government and restored an imperial system in its place, Japan started to embark on an industrial revolution of its own. Eventually, the nation became an electrical powerhouse. This can be traced back to how, unlike some other countries in East Asia, Japan did not fear that the importation of new Western technologies would also necessitate the importation of new Western values. Rather, they welcomed Western ideas into their technical education, even employing Britain's telegraph

---

[3] Lang, "Lightning Wires," 354.

[4] Lang, "Lightning Wires," 355.

[5] Lang, "Lightning Wires," 355.

system in 1869, France's judicial system in 1872, and the United States's primary school education system in 1879.[6] As it relates to electricity specifically, Son quotes Neil Pedlar, author of "The Imported Pioneers, Westerners Who Helped Build Modern Japan," to further establish this acceptance of Western technology in terms of Japanese electrical engineers:

With no ancient traditions to uphold, … almost fanatical support for Westernization, … and believing whole-heartedly in … embracing many innovations, the Imperial College of Engineering became the most advanced institution of its kind in the world.[7]

Such adoption, modification, and absorption of foreign ideologies and technologies into Japanese daily life subsequently contributed to dramatic innovation-based growth in Japan, both from foreign influence and domestic originations, during the late nineteenth and early twentieth centuries.

Europe and the United States

Just as it is important to consider the comparisons of electrification in Korea to that of China and Japan, it would be remiss to not also include a brief analysis of electricity in the West to situate electrical Korea on a broader global timeline. The existing European and American literature on this topic is additionally instructive as current academic investigations into Western science address the differences not only among East Asian countries and Western countries, but also the critical distinctions even within Western nations, as well. It becomes clear that by openly sharing scientific knowledge across the West by means of extensive travel and constant dialogue, one 'standard' path toward technological modernization, even in the West, does not exist.

Electricity as it is known today was pioneered in the West by a collection of renowned scientists including Ben Franklin of America, Alessandro Volta of Italy, and Michael Faraday of Britain. These electrical engineers took a mysterious scientific entity and turned it into something both fathomable and useful. Born in the age of the American Enlightenment, Franklin valued democratic culture and sought out a science that would both educate and elevate American society. His curiosity led him to prove the existence of positive and negative electric charges in

---

[6] Tom Nicholas, "The Origins of Japanese Technological Modernization," Explorations in Economic History (2011): 273.

[7] Min Suh Son, "Electrifying Seoul and the Culture of Technology," PhD diss., (University of California, 2006), 13.

the mid 1700s, and later he went on to work with experimenters in both England and France to develop the Leyden jar and lightning rod.[8] In 1800, Volta invented the voltaic cell which made it possible to power electrical devices using relatively low voltages and high currents, subsequently influencing the development of the European telegraph.[9] Then, in 1831, Faraday discovered the scientific relationship between electricity and magnetism, thus spurring a new wave of mechanical examinations of electric currents and the application of said currents in the development of electric motors, light sources, and communication devices across Britain.[10] Each western country studied, developed, and implemented electrical technologies in different ways; the expansion of electricity throughout the West was therefore not solely dominated by just one single country of origin—rather, electrical knowledge was freely and enthusiastically transferred among Europe and the United States to be implemented as each nation saw fit.[11] By the early twentieth century, nearly all cities across the West were vying to become electrified, reflecting a culture that idealized an electrical utopia.

Historical Account of Electricity in Korea

Evidently, scholars in the past have put an emphasis on studying the functionality of electricity, and how its utility has served a necessary purpose for society throughout the last two centuries. Rather than solely focusing on electrical functionality in Korea, however, I dive into the complex relationship between electrical technology and Korean culture by closely examining how innovative electrical tools themselves can act as a node to connect Korean culture, politics, and people in new ways over time.

Defining Kaehwa

Such technological transformation toward modernization first began in Seoul, Korea during the late nineteenth century, when American engineers arrived to install the first lighting system.[12] Because Western science had the reputation of

---

[8] Robert Angus Buchanan, "History of Technology," Britannica, November 18, https://www.britannica.com/technology/history-of-technology.

[9] Buchanan, "History of Technology."

[10] Buchanan, "History of Technology."

[11] Son, "Electrifying Seoul," 15.

[12] Son, "Electrifying Seoul," 24.

being the measure of a civilization's ultimate success, Korea initially embraced American technology as a vehicle for making their society appear more culturally, politically, and technologically advanced.[13] These progressive Korean reformers identified as the *kaehwa*, Korean for "civilization and enlightenment," and believed in implementing Korean reforms modeled after socio-political institutions throughout the West.[14] By way of accepting the superiority of Western technology while also preserving Korean traditions, however, *kaehwa* scientists and engineers needed to study electricity abroad first-hand.

1800s: Studying Western Ideology and Traveling Abroad

During this Korean enlightenment period, the intellectual experimentation and adaptation of electricity led *kaehwa* inventors to contemplate how to merge new ideas of the West with contemporary adaptations from Japan and China in order to emerge with influential electrical innovations of their own. Such a process of Korean electrification required either academic missions abroad or a domestic study of translated scientific writings from China and Japan. At first, missions abroad were only an option for the Korean elite, as expeditions to study a relatively unvetted science remained too expensive for the government to support. Scholars and engineers alike consequently started reading about Western electrical advancement, with a particular focus on how China and Japan implemented these new and somewhat abstract electrical technologies into East Asia. Literature included writings from Confucian scholar Wei Yuan, Chinese missionary Benjamin Hobson, and Japanese technology blueprints.[15] Once these scientific texts began to circulate among Korean scholars, it was not long before interest in Western scientific inquiry spread across the nation.

The Chosŏn government's decision to finally support scientific missions abroad was therefore twofold: (1) Korea wanted to improve their relations with their East Asian neighbors in China and Japan, and (2) scholars hoped to learn more about Western technological institutions. While two previous missions to Japan in 1876 and 1880 were mainly diplomatic in character, the mission in 1881 to Japan had an emphasis on observing the modernization practices undertaken by the Meiji government. Nicknamed the "Gentlemen's Observation Mission," scientists,

---

[13] Michael Adas, *Machines as the Measure of Men: Science, Technology, and Ideologies of Western Dominance*, 1. (Ithaca: Cornell University Press), 133.

[14] Son, "Electrifying Seoul," 25.

[15] Son, "Electrifying Seoul," 31.

philosophers, politicians, and activists alike such as Yu Kilchun, Yun Ch'iho, Hong Yŏngsik, Ŏ Yunjung, Pak Chŏngyang, and Cho Chunyŏng embarked on a three month fact-finding mission to Japan.[16]

A consequence of this mission was the disagreements that emerged among *kaehwa* reformers on how to implement Western technologies into Korean technological reform. In Son's examination, she recognized that an account of this mission can be composed of remaining primary source documents such as the official royal report, Kang Munhyong's "Records from Japan," and Yi Wonhui and Song Honbin's "Tokyo Journal." After conducting a deep analysis of these documents, focusing on their direct references to science and technology specifically, Son determined that to the majority of Korean travelers, Japan's modernization efforts were highly flawed.[17] Because many expeditioners viewed Japan through the lens of Korean superiority, they were thrown off by the financial debt faced by the Meiji government and the influx of Westernized culture following the introduction of Western technologies. As such, their experiences in Japan led them to oppose the pursuit of similar reforms in Korea.

For younger *kaehwa* members on the voyage, on the other hand, Meiji restoration served as an enticing prototype for the technological restructuring of Korea. They argued that the adoption of Western technologies would not only present a palpable solution for military defense against foreign invasion, but also that Westernization as a whole would elevate Korea's national position as a modernized, and therefore "civilized," country.[18] Yet even among these *kaehwa* modernizers, there was a range in technological philosophy. While some pushed for a slow political radicalization that attempted to harmonize both Western and Korean ideologies, others pursued a more thorough rejection of traditional Korean values. The latter argued for complete "Westernization—including Western political institutions, Christianity, new technologies—to displace Neo-Confucianism as Korea's cultural and political foundation."[19] Because of these great disagreements among travelers returning from Japan, the Korean government was prompted to administer another observation mission, this time to China.

---

[16] Son, "Electrifying Seoul," 31.

[17] Son, "Electrifying Seoul," 32.

[18] Adas, *Machines as the Measure of Men*, 140.

[19] Son, "Electrifying Seoul," 35.

The *Yŏngsŏnsa* mission to China in 1882 involved sending Korean students to enroll in schools in Beijing and Shanghai. In doing so, the Korean government hoped the students could actively educate and implement the new electrical curricula into Korea upon their return.[20] Apart from the educational aspect of this Korean quest, King Kojong concurrently intended on learning about new Westernized military technologies in China. In order to achieve this dual understanding of both educational and technological modernization, Korea sent about 80 travelers on the trip, including officials, students, and staff.[21] Unfortunately, the mission in China was cut short due to the Imo Incident in Seoul during July of 1882, but the Korean scholars did return from China with a greater understanding and appreciation for Westernization than they had before. Once back in Korea, the students and officials put into practice the knowledge they had acquired. Working with the government, they constructed a machine warehouse, electric network, modern transport system, and communications infrastructure in Seoul inspired by what they had observed in China. Such Korean innovations therefore led to the modernization and electrification of the city.

Up to 1882, Korea had largely acquired its understanding of Western knowledge and technological institutions via these excursions to China and Japan. As a result, Korea's view of Westernization was primarily shaped by Chinese ideas of *haebang* (overcoming Western powers by learning and implementing them) and *yangmu* (learning from the West), as well as the Japanese philosophy of *bunmei-kaika* (Western civilization in terms of enlightenment ideals).[22] Such planned encounters with Western knowledge from the Korean government were therefore prone to many misunderstandings due to obvious mistranslations from nation to nation. So, as the largest metropolis in Korea officially started to become electrified, the Chosŏn government opted for one last technologically and politically motivated voyage to the United States. In what became the largest expedition yet, diplomats Min Yŏngik and Sŏ Kwangbŏm led the mission to Washington DC, San Francisco, New York, and Boston.[23] While the primary purpose of this trip was to secure both economic support and diplomatic recognition from the United States in order to strengthen Chosŏn's national independence, the mission was also

---

[20] Son, "Electrifying Seoul," 35.

[21] Son, "Electrifying Seoul," 36.

[22] Young-Sin Park, "The Chosŏn Industrial Exposition of 1915," PhD diss., (Graduate School of Binghamton University, 2019), 47.

[23] Gary D. Walter, "The Korean Special Mission to the United States of America in 1883," *Journal of Korean Studies* 1, 1 (1969): 101.

necessary as it gave Korean officials the ability to observe the West and its electrical advancements directly, separate from Japanese or Chinese interpretation. In Japan, Korean diplomats were exposed only to a vague exhibition of Western electricity, as it was still being developed there. China was the same. The mission to the United States, however, gave members the ability to visit vibrantly electrified farms, factories, banks, hospitals, schools, and more:

On Wednesday afternoon the Coreans visited the United States Electric Light Company. They were accompanied by Mr. Hebard, President of the company, and a car was placed at their disposal by the Superintendent of the Delaware, Lackawanna and Western Railroad. The Coreans were initiated into the manufacture of electricity from the beginning to the end. They inspected the testing machines and lamps under Mr. Western's charge.[24]

With this first-hand exposure to the production of electricity, Korean scholars became "emboldened with the sense that they had the ability to harness this energy on their own."[25] Such electrical influences inspired Min Yŏngik to plan a great international industrial exposition upon his return to Seoul, Korea, a projection of both his national identity and acknowledgment of Western modern advancement.[26]

As a result of all three of these missions, plus a growing domestic interest in electricity within Korea, the electrification and industrial development of Seoul quickly became a primary way to preserve national sovereignty. For example, the electric light, introduced in 1887, illuminated the city and specially represented a greatly prosperous and modernized Korea. Its installation was the result of three key factors: the unique properties of electrical networks, competition against other modernizing countries, and the commercial ambitions of American inventor Thomas Edison.[27] It is no surprise, then, that the electric light attracted more scientific interest than any other technological breakthrough. Cheaper, lighter, and safer than gas or kerosene, it was used on public streets and within homes.[28] Following its widespread introduction to Seoul, the city immediately became much more vibrant, providing a newfound nightlife that created a valued freedom

---

[24] "Coreans Seeing the Sights; Interested in the Manufacture of Silk and Electricity," *New York Times* (1883).

[25] Son, "Electrifying Seoul," 38.

[26] Park, "Chosŏn Industrial Exposition," 49.

[27] Son, "Electrifying Seoul," 40.

[28] Son, "Electrifying Seoul," 2.

to safely move, work, and entertain. Residents stayed out later, worked longer hours, and explored the city streets with a greater sense of security. The light consequently "transformed conventional notions of time, extending usable hours for work and socializing which contributed to the rise of new forms of entertainment and social gathering."[29] Metropolises were being reimagined.

1900s: Korea's Technological Boom

Electricity in Korea reached new heights at the turn of the twentieth century. While the Japanese government had only begun to consider the implications of electricity beyond simply lighting up the night, Korean electrical development was already well on its way to implementing its own telegraph and streetcar system. Such practical technologies enabled the easy transmission of dialogue and provided much quicker transportation options for Korean residents. Subsequently, electricity, both literally and metaphorically, was able to successfully bridge the gap between individuals all over Korea and beyond. Such new technological abilities thereby supported the notion of human interconnectedness and community on a local and global scale, linking Korea beyond its borders to Japan, China, Russia and the Western hemisphere.[30] The telegraph in particular allowed Koreans to both communicate instantaneously overseas, as well as elevate their global position in the commercial economic space. Yet for Koreans, the successful integration of Western technology into daily life provided much more than just utility. For them, to be modernized was to be enlightened and civilized, among the relative ranks of Europe and the United States. Both industrial advancement and electrical research and development thus played significant roles in establishing national independence and international respect. It can be inferred, then, that electricity provided so much more than simply a technological function—it acted as a catalyst for the legal, political, and social restructuring of Korea throughout the nineteenth and into the twentieth century.

The desire to keep inventing new electrical technologies in Korea did not falter. Despite political turmoil in the early to mid 1900s, when Korean sovereignty fell to Japanese annexation, the domestic drive for modernization still persisted. In the early 1910s, Japanese scholars continued knowledge production and electrical innovation in order to legitimize its hold on Korea. Despite its often oppressive rule, recognizable modern aspects of Korean society emerged from Japan's

---

[29] Son, "Electrifying Seoul," 3.

[30] *IBID.*

occupation such as the radio and popular cinema. In 1927, the radio industry in particular really took off, with 725 of the 1114 nationwide radio receivers found in the heart of Seoul. [31] Providing both entertainment and education, radio programing included academic lectures, book readings, concerts featuring Korean and Japanese artists, plays, comedy, and more.[32] It notably reached both Japanese and Korean audiences, and restructured the way in which residents received their information. By 1945, the number of radios nationwide reached a quarter of a million; the news of liberation from Japanese colonial rule thereby came to many via wireless. [33] And that number of listeners only increased afterwards.

Additionally, Japanese authorities placed an emphasis on industrial development in Korea, although motives to do so were primarily for the purposes of enriching the Japanese economy and military rule over China, not for the prosperity of Koreans themselves. It makes sense, then, that many of the industrial programs employed by the Japanese government in Korea during the 1920s and 1930s actually originated from policies drafted, but never enforced, in Japan during the Meiji period. [34] Under Japanese rule, the Korean economy underwent a considerable transformation. Korea's traditional primary industry of agriculture shrank from its original 70% to 40% of GDP, meanwhile the relative proportion of industries in mining and manufacturing grew from about 5% to 20% of the total economy.[35] Such a rapid transition from a primarily agricultural economy to a primarily non-agricultural one was a direct result of Western modernization techniques and yet another distinct example of the restructuring of daily life in Korea due to electrical developments. By the time the Japanese surrendered in 1945, Korea was ranked as the second-most industrialized nation in all of Asia.

The Korean electrical grid to this day still relies on the faculties built by Japan during their colonial rule. As such, by the late twentieth century, South Korea was reasonably modernized with a strong nationalistic urge to invest in technological development. From roughly 1950 to 1990, during the Cold War, electrification

---

[31] Andrei Lankov, "Who Listened to the Radio?," The Korea Times, July 10, 2009, http://www.koreatimes.co.kr/www/nation/2018/07/165_48243.html.

[32] Lankov, "Who Listened to the Radio?"

[33] *IBID.*

[34] Andrea Matles Savada and William Shaw, South Korea: A Country Study, (Washington, D.C.: Federal Research Division, Library of Congress, 1992).

[35] Mitsuhiko Kimura, "Colonial Development of Modern Industry in Korea, 1910-1939/40," Korea Under the Rule of Japan: What Statistics and Empirical Research Tell Us (2018): 23.

was actively dominated by the national Korean government. [36] Because of electricity's central role in both industrialization efforts and residential standards, it necessitated such authoritarian control. During this time, the government employed various economic five year plans that included four primary electrically motivated advances: (1) constructing thermal plants across the South, (2) working directly with the power provider Korean Electric Power Company (KEPCO), (3) employing an electronics industry promotion strategy, and (4) restricting foreign product imports.[37] As a result of these conscious efforts, electrical industries within Korea rapidly grew at a much faster rate than its foreign counterparts, suggesting that this important switch in governmental policy and corporate strategy was highly effective at establishing a scientific presence, national confidence, and cultural pride.

Electricity as a Marker for Korean Progress

Electricity in Korea is therefore so much more than simply a practical necessity of industrialization and modernization. It has also continued to play a vital role in creating and supporting a strong national ideology, one which represents an important social tie between its country and its citizens. [38] The electrical technologies I examined here are a reflection of this sentiment. While electricity's gradual implementation into Korea did force officials to consider significant issues of modern binaries—Westernization versus tradition, nationalism versus global cooperation, technological progress versus conventional backwardness, scientific rationalism versus religious superstition—the telegraph, electric light, and radio are all ultimately examples of how electricity, when placed in the Korean space, subsequently restructured, and thus illuminated, the culture around its existence.

---

[36] James H. Williams and Navroz K. Dubash, "Asian Electricity Reform in Historical Perspective," The Political Economy of Electricity Reform in Asia 77, 3 (2004): 411.

[37] John P. Dimoia, ""Difficult Heritage" & Selective Elision: The Seoul Power Plant," Technology and Culture (2021): 561.

[38] James H. Williams and Navroz K. Dubash, "Asian Electricity Reform," 412.

Redefining Korean Innovation in Science Fiction: A Survey of the Dolly in Moving Image

Leandra Djomo

Abstract

Korean cinema has always been praised for its artful cinematography and storytelling capabilities. However, Korean movies and TV Shows have not achieved a groundbreaking track record in other international industries. In fact, many #1 box-office hits in South Korea were American films, demonstrating the position of the Korean film industry. A drastic shift in Korean film aesthetics helped filmmakers grasp the concept of glocalization–the notion of taking global influences and connecting them with local preferences. The change in cinematography is accredited to film technology in Korean films and their use of these advanced technologies to produce transnational media. In particular, the Korean zombie genre and the industry's goals to expand Korean science fiction increased the appeal towards Korean apocalyptic media from both global and local audiences. By examining *Kingdom* (2019) from director Kim Seong-hun, this paper seeks to understand the role of the dolly as a cinematographic film technology in marketing Korean science fiction internationally through the use of the tracking shot. Further, I will analyze the history of the tracking shot to discuss its specific use in Korean cinema to determine its part in positioning the Korean film industry as one of the top industries today. How does dolly technology advance Korean cinema to global popularity? The presence of a niche audience dedicated to the zombie genre and the firm use of glocalization by Korean directors dictate the status of Korean science fiction and Korean cinema worldwide.

Introduction

Over the past decade, South Korean cinema gained global popularity due to the captivating storylines in its films and TV shows. Fans also discuss the impact of contemporary cinematography in Korean cinema; however, the effect of film technology in Korean films is rarely discussed among American scholars. The growing interest in Korean apocalyptic shows and movies from audiences abroad demonstrates the effective use of film technology to create media that resonates universally rather than just locally. Kim Seong-hun (1971-present) complicates the audience's understanding of film technology in the hit Netflix series *Kingdom* (2019) by showing the importance of a tracking shot and how it helps narrate the plot.

The Korean film industry supposedly attained traction overseas due to its stylistic use of the tracking shot. I acknowledge that the attraction towards Korean media by foreign consumers is in part because of the distribution of Korean films through digital technologies. Netflix, as a streaming service, contributes to the international spread of Korean cinema with its recent growing filmography of original Korean shows. In particular, *Kingdom* presents itself as a political drama, thriller, and horror series. The plot follows people from the Chosŏn period who are plagued by a "resurrection herb" which turns people into invincible zombies.

Thus, the aim of this paper is to demonstrate how *Kingdom* uses the dolly technology to produce realistic shots that frame the show as science fiction. This paper will look at the history of the tracking shot and its importance in film, and how the use of a tracking shot in apocalyptic Korean media has led the genre to worldwide acclaim. What is the role of film technology in advancing one's discernment of Korean science fiction and horror? How do digital technologies such as Netflix help Korean cinema reach global audiences? Expanding on Barry Salt's analysis of the tracking shot as a tool used to capture movement in film, I will examine how the tracking shot blurs the line between fiction and reality by creating a genuine fear in audiences when watching science fiction. Furthermore, I will argue the effect of film technology as a tool that has a social impact amongst global audiences.

Glocalization and the Korean Zombie Craze

Korean cinema did not always have the global mass following it has today. In the case of science-fiction (hereafter sci-fi), many early 2000s blockbusters in the genre did not financially recover from box-office sales resulting in profit loss.[1] This loss proves a local disinterest in sci-fi from Korean audiences. Per Kim in his analysis of sci-fi in South Korea, what constricted this genre in the nation was Confucian tradition that opposed the concepts of science and technology and that screenwriters did not take the time to consult scientists and engineers to construct an accurate portrayal of sci-fi.[2] However, Korea still became the "fifth largest theatrical market in the world" by 2005.[3] By the start of the 21st century, the Korean film industry saw a shift in the production of its films as well as their narratives. Korean directors began adopting Hollywood film practices while maintaining appeal towards local audiences through topics such as "national identity, class mobility, gender, and sexuality".[4] Despite borrowing from these aesthetics, Korean directors have more creative freedom in making their own scripts, giving them the chance to experiment with their films, while "the Hollywood industry often bases its films on presold properties: best-sellers, comics, plays, tv shows, or well-known historical events".[5] Due to Hollywood's significant status as a film industry giant for cinephiles around the world, the borrowed artistic characteristics from Hollywood found in Korean cinema lure in global audiences. Yet, the topics that cater to Korean audiences are unfamiliar to global spectators and these aspects act as another tool to engage foreign consumers.

The hybrid structure Korean directors use to develop Korean cinema by adopting stylistic elements from other national cinemas while retaining local attraction is known as glocalization. Keith B. Wagner defines glocalization in the context of Korean cinema as bringing "the global, in the sense of the macroscopic aspects of

---

[1] Choi, Jin-hee, The South Korean Film Renaissance: Local Hitmakers, Global Provocateurs, Wesleyan University Press, 2010, 35.

[2] Kim, Dong-Won, "Science Fiction in South and North Korea- Reading Science and Technology as Fantasized in Cultures," East Asian Science, Technology and Society: An International Journal, 2018, 12:309–326
DOI 10.1215/18752160-6975882, 312.

[3] *IBID*, 2.

[4] *IBID*, 11.

[5] *IBID*, 37.

contemporary life into conjunction with the local".[6] My purpose in focusing on Wagner's interpretation of glocalization serves to clarify that global attraction towards Korean media is not due to a sole interest in Korean culture nor a familiarity with Hollywood aesthetics; rather, both components are necessary in defining contemporary Korean filmography. Despite a desire to interchange interest between global and local spectators by developing glocalization in their films, "Korean directors exploit national identity and national history in order to reach out to a wider audience".[7] However, the content of their work is not necessarily nationalistic, nor does it exclude non-Koreans from engaging with important themes in the narratives. Yet, Jin Dal-yong insists that through the "asymmetrical interplay between global and local forces, the Korean film industry has lost its strong position as a concrete and independent Third World Cinema".[8] Although the global influence on Korean filmmaking is apparent, it would be disingenuous to agree that Korea has lost its strong position in film because of its use of other cinemas. Glocalization has helped the nation further develop a film identity that is unique to Korea. Other cinemas may also be able to adapt the notion of glocalization, nevertheless that does not mean that their cinemas are not distinctive. To utilize glocalization precisely would be to recognize the indispensable need for local forces which is what makes Korean cinema unmistakably Korean.

The zombie, apocalyptic subgenre is ideal in further understanding the notion of glocalization in the Korean film industry. The zombie category is well-documented in Hollywood's history and is attributed to American cinema. The zombie genre fits into the definition of sci-fi as stated by Kim: "fiction in which the setting and story feature hypothetical scientific or technological advances, the existence of alien life, space or time travel, etc., esp. such fiction set in the future, or an imagined alternative universe".[9] The zombies in films are specimens of alien life as they are foreigners who do not belong with the humans in society. Despite the genre's establishment in the American film industry, "cultural anxiety or even feelings of dread are also tied to the ways in which South Korea and societies

---

[6] Wagner, Keith B, "*Train to Busan* (2016): Glocalization, Korean Zombies, and Man-made Neoliberal Disaster," *Rediscovering Korean Cinema*, edited by Sang-joon Lee, University of Michigan Press, 2019, 515.

[7] Choi, *South Korean Film Renaissance*, 58.

[8] Jin, Dal-yong, *Transnational Korean Cinema: Cultural Politics, Film Genres, and Digital Technologies*, Rutgers University Press, 2020, 150.

[9] Kim, Dong-Won, *East Asian Science*, 310.

worldwide now operate on a level of mere socioeconomic survival".[10] Thus, the Korean zombie category gained a global mass following because it created a relation between foreign consumers and a shared experience of cultural anxiety worldwide. Additionally, "South Korean science fiction is not very futuristic [as most] works describe the very near future, one or two generations beyond the present; very few deal with society in the far-distant future."[11] Korea's success in the zombie genre is because it concerns itself with present-day issues that threaten the future. There is then no need for South Korean sci-fi screenwriters to go temporally beyond in their storytelling as the idea of zombies fits the current framing of sci-fi in Korea. How does the Korean zombie category appease transnational cultural anxiety while preserving contemporary Korean film trends?

Glocalization gives Korean directors a solution to incorporating particular stylistic choices in their films while continuing to create films for a Korean audience and increasingly switching aesthetics to obtain a wider audience outside the country. To maintain balance in this hybrid structure, Korean zombie media guarantees features of "Koreaness" in the appearance of the zombies: universally, zombie actors' makeup consists of "whitened irises, veiny and blanched faces covered in mucus, flesh particles and blackened blood spatter, and bodies hunched over and in various stages of decay and decrepitude".[12] However, the use of an "Asian-only cast of zombies [...] [establishes] a Korean-only zombie film".[13] Monoracial casting in Korean zombie media could be mistaken as a case of nationalism from the director. Monoracial casting in Korean zombie media is necessary to maintain the balance in glocalization; so, monoracial casting in this instance keeps the standards needed for the local audience to enjoy a traditionally un-Korean genre. For example, the characters in *Kingdom* "enjoy traditional Korean foods, speak Korean slang, spout Korean proverbs, and remember past stories that only Koreans would understand".[14] These features are distinctly for Korean audiences to appreciate, but unknown to outside viewers.

Further, after a review of Wagner's recent scholarship on cultural anxiety in their analysis of *Train to Busan* (2016) by Yeon Sang-ho (1978-present), I consider how digital technology relates to science-fiction as factors to promote Korean cinema

---

[10] Wagner, *Rediscovering Korean Cinema*, 516.

[11] Kim, Dong-Won, *East Asian Science*, 310.

[12] Wagner, *Rediscovering Korean Cinema*, 522.

[13] *IBID.*

[14] Kim, Dong-Won, *East Asian Science*, 323.

globally. As Jin argues, Netflix as a digital technology played an important role in recent years in growing Korean cinema.[15] Regardless of the growth of Korean cinema, Jin claims that it has yet to build a strong existence within transnational cinema but adds that a significant presence can be created as "contemporary Korean cinema is increasingly dependent on digital platforms and storytelling—from production to distribution to exhibition".[16] While I agree with the latter point that Korean cinema will see exponential growth if it continues exploiting digital technologies, Korean cinema garnered a noteworthy reputation in the global film industry. Jin's scholarship on transnational cinema came out in December 2019, while *Kingdom* and *Parasite* by Bong Joon-ho respectively came out in the first half of 2019. These two medias are perfect examples showcasing the new global success of Korean cinema. So, for the author to not account for their impact in inaugurating a new era for the Korean film industry internationally is unexpected. Nonetheless, with or without the emergence of digital technologies, Korean directors are still required to depend on film technologies to emulate the Hollywood aesthetics they strive for to obtain global recognition.

Overview of the Dolly Technology

To acquire "aesthetic elevation"[17] Korean directors need to work with their cinematographers to adequately make use of film technologies to achieve their stylistic goals. These directors are personally involved in the screenwriting process[18] and therefore have an advantage in exploring their creativeness when it comes to increasing aesthetics. As per Enticknap in his analysis of moving image technology:

> *Cinematography, which can broadly be defined as the technology needed to expose photographic images (or 'frames') onto film which are intended to be reproduced as a moving image sequence, consists primarily of the cameras themselves and the peripheral technologies designed to facilitate their use (such as studio lighting).[19]*

---

[15] Jin, Dal-yong, Transnational Korean Cinema, 156.

[16] *IBID.*

[17] Choi, South Korean Film Renaissance, 58.

[18] *IBID,* 22.

[19] Enticknap, Leo, Moving Image Technology: From Zoetrope to Digital (London: Wallflower, 2005), 29.

Accordingly, cinematography in and of itself is a technological medium that is made up of different physical machines to create visual and auditory moving art. The dolly is a film technology that produces the tracking shot (a camera movement) and an essential part of contemporary cinematography. A tracking shot is made by placing a camera on a dolly which then follows a subject through space to create a smooth shot.[20] The tracking shot can be found in all genres as it is a foundational film technique that enhances the cinematography of a film. Barry Salt claims that the tracking shot has a technological role in creating film style which shows how film technologies also affect Korean cinema and aid in the development of its distinct stylistic choices through the lens of sci-fi.

The dolly is a camera support that moves on tracks "to show a view of a more or less static scene from the front of a moving vehicle".[21] The dolly as a camera support comes in different improvised forms such as forklift trucks, cranes, or other platforms, which make "possible limited camera rises combined with a tracking movement".[22] Historically, the dolly has always been used to produce tracking shots as early as 1903, but only to track objects. The first encounter of a dolly being used on actors to create a tracking shot is in the 1914 Italian film *Cabiria* by Giovanni Pastrone (1888-1959) known as '*Cabiria* movements' in the film industry. The use of the dolly in this context was intended to "create a 'three-dimensional' effect in the photography to show off the vast solid sets of his film, and for this reason his tracking shots were made moving inwards on a diagonal" per Pastrone.[23] Pastrone can be credited as the inventor of the tracking shot via dolly technology and its ample use on actors as seen in modern cinema today. Salt acknowledges the existence of the dolly technology prior to Pastrone's significant use of it in film technology history. However, can Pastrone be accredited as the inventor of this particular use of the dolly? Or was he solely innovative in his exploration of this technology and how does this apply to Korean society and their technological advancements within the film industry?

In his investigation of technological film history, Gomery furthers the discussion surrounding the role of technology in cinema. Quoting Edwin Mansfield, Gomery defines invention as "a prescription for a new product or process that was not

---

20 Dirks, Tim, Film Terms Glossary. "Film Terms Glossary: pan (or panning shot, or panoramic shot)". filmsite.org.

21 Salt, Barry, Film Style and Technology: History and Analysis (London: Starword, 1983), 50.

22 *Ibid*, 203.

23 *Ibid*, 138.

obvious to one skilled in the relevant art at the time the idea was generated".[24] I argue that Pastrone was an inventor of the specific use of the dolly technology that constructs the tracking shot involving actors. However, the same cannot be said for the use of the tracking shot in Korean cinema. Choi Hyung-sub's scholarship on imported technologies in Korea demonstrates how Korean scholars diverted from only studying things unique to Korea; they were "compelled to leave out much of the scientific activities conducted within the geographical confines of the Korean peninsula that lack perceivable differences with those in [other nations]".[25]

Thus, when looking at the conditions that shaped contemporary Korean cinema, it can be inferred that "'Korean-style' [film] technologies"[26] are not inventions but innovations, despite Choi mentioning that Korean society "lacked significant experiences in technological innovation".[27] The concept of Korean directors being innovators rather than inventors when it comes to film technology such as the dolly and its various uses is proven by the implementation of glocalization within Korean cinema. Korean directors make use of "their continued experiences with new hybrid cultural forms"[28] to become more innovative with their stylistic choices in their films, which attracts foreign consumers. Furthermore, Gomery defines innovation as "a system of inventions [adopted] for practical use"[29] which involves "a firm altering [of] past methods of production, distribution, and for marketing because [innovation] has determined that the adoption of the invention will result in greater long-term profits".[30] The profits of the innovative contemporary Korean cinema reflects the industry becoming "one of the strongest commercial film industries in the region, outperforming Hollywood cinema at the local box office" in recent years.[31]

An example of innovative use of the tracking shot in Korean cinema is with director Song Il-gon (1971-present), the first Korean filmmaker who won an

---

[24] Gomery, Douglas, Film History: Theory and Practice (New York: Knopf, 1985), 114.

[25] Choi, Hyung-sub, "The Social Construction of Imported Technologies: Reflections on the Social History of Technology in Modern Korea," Technology and Culture, Volume 58, Number 4, Johns Hopkins University Press, October 2017, 910, DOI: https://doi.org/10.1353/tech.2017.0108, 910.

[26] *IBID*, 915.

[27] *IBID*, 909.

[28] Wagner, Rediscovering Korean Cinema, 521.

[29] Gomery, Film History, 114.

[30] *IBID*.

[31] Choi, South Korean Film Renaissance, 1.

award at the Cannes Film Festival. Song directed *The Magicians* (2005), a 40-minute movie lengthened into 96 minutes, all done in one tracking shot.[32] Although Song is not the inventor of the tracking shot, he takes the dolly technology to greater lengths by experimenting with the tracking shot and playing with the limits of the camera movements with this one film technique. By doing so, Song generates a continued temporal setting in his film which gives it a slow pace. Song shows how the dolly can alter the tone of a film as well as its aesthetics. This modification through film technology has weight in determining the success of a film amongst audiences.

Kingdom as a Case Study

Kingdom is available on Netflix worldwide and was well received in the West as well as regionally in countries surrounding Korea [33] thanks to the astounding cinematography and the show's ability to "[intersperse] social realism with monster gore".[34] Due to its high demand, the show has two seasons which came out in 2019 and 2020, and a special episode called *Kingdom: Ashin of the North*, also directed by Kim Seong-hun which came out in the summer of 2021. The series' plot shows how the "resurrection herb" was used as a quick solution to defeat the Japanese invaders which led to the execution and burial of the zombies. However, the plant emerged again to feign the existence of the dead king to ensure that the prince–conceived from a concubine–would not take the throne. Instead, the governors waited for the king's daughter, the queen, to produce a son. Their selfish deeds caused the plant-based disease outbreak. The large-scale human error of disseminating this virus, the presence of zombies, and the Korean-only characters position *Kingdom* as a typical Korean sci-fi series.

As contended by Wagner, the zombies in *Kingdom* have the appearance common to most international zombie films, however, young audiences can relate to the show having young survivors of the virus outbreak who live in a "complete destruction of society, out of which a post-apocalyptic world emerges".[35] The

---

[32] Kim, Tae-jong (2 May 2005). "Freer Expression Thru Digital Media". The Korea Times.

[33] David Opie, Sam Ashurst, Tilly Pearce, "Kingdom Season 3 Potential Release Date, Cast, Plot, and Everything You Need to Know," Digital Spy, 2022, https://www.digitalspy.com/tv/a31669844/kingdom-season-3-release-date-netflix/

[34] Wagner, Rediscovering Korean Cinema, 516.

[35] *IBID*, 526.

show uses disaster narratives (such as disease) that can occur anywhere in the world to create a parallel between a Korean-only zombie film with a non-Korean audience.[36] Through the analysis of tracking shots in the first season of *Kingdom,* elements of sci-fi and horror will be exhibited by emphasizing the dolly technology as an vital tool in the cinematography of the series and a factor in generating global success.

In the first episode of the series, the audience sees two people from the king's court walking towards his room to serve him his dinner. The eldest servant warns the younger one that he must not look into the king's bedchamber. The younger servant makes the mistake of looking inside, is dragged, and presumably eaten by the diseased king.[37] Following this scene is a series of tracking shots that heighten the gruesome atmosphere while giving the audience a glimpse of the disease's consequences. Shot 1[38] uses the dolly technology backwards to show the door to the king's bedroom. This backwards dolly movement is continued in Shot 2[39] where the audience sees the corner the two court servants turned to get to the king's chamber. In Shot 3[40], the camera movement now depicts the whole of the king's house in the same backwards motion, with the sound of the young servant screaming for his life in the background throughout all three shots, and slowly fading out as the camera slowly removes itself from the cannibalistic home. These shots establish the tone of the first episode as one filled with suspense and fear from the knowledge that the virus is amongst the highest ranks of society; so, the virus rendered even the king useless which puts the rest of the population at risk for catching the disease in addition to living with a disordered governing body. This fear is exacerbated in Shot 4[41] through a forward dolly movement presenting a poster that reads "The king is dead. A new wind will blow." [왕은 죽었다. 새로운 바람이 불 것이다.]. This message foreshadows the consequences of the king's inability to lead the nation and the start of the spread of the disease. Another tracking shot is used in Shot 5[42], the last shot of the episode, to reveal the impending doom that was insinuated in Shot 4. The scene preceding Shot 5 shows

---

[36] *IBID,* 522.

[37] Kim, Seong Hun, director. 2019. Kingdom. Netflix.

[38] (Kim 2019, 05:32-05:33)

[39] (Kim 2019, 05:33-05:34)

[40] (Kim 2019, 05:36-05:44)

[41] (Kim 2019, 05:50-05:54)

[42] (Kim 2019, 52:00-52:13)

a male and female protagonist arguing because the man fed a human corpse to the unknowing villagers on account of the scarcity of food and a demand for meat. A woman physician berates him on his decision in a shed away from the villagers who are gradually succumbing to the disease that was in the cooked corpse. Shot 5 shows the entrance to the village as the camera is moved forward on the dolly to a crack in the wooden door where the audience sees fire and zombies running frantically, until one zombie runs directly towards that same door crack while screeching, creating a doomsday-like atmosphere for the viewers.

Although the shots analyzed here are not the classic tracking shots following the movement of actors, they are still tracking shots that clearly present the purpose of the dolly as a powerful technology to elevate the aesthetics in the cinematography of a media. Producing good aesthetics is critical in helping the Korean film industry to manufacture genuine interest from foreign consumers. Further, to do so in a niche genre of zombie films known to be Hollywood's expertise is to expand the perception of what Korean cinema is and what it can accomplish.

Conclusion

South Korean cinema has made a reputation for itself by modifying the aesthetics in its cinematography while still providing cultural content for a local audience through the concept of glocalization. In particular, the Korean film industry used existing film technologies to elevate the cinematography in their media. The dolly technology was not the overall cause for Korean cinema's and the zombie genre's global success; but the dolly is part of cinematography, and it is cinematographic aesthetics that determined international acclaim. The scholarship on film technology is effective in providing a detailed account of the creation of important film technologies, how they are used, and what their purpose is. In particular, Barry Salt examines the use of film technologies in notable movies while also looking at improvisations of said technologies to highlight stylistic developments in his book "Film Style and Technology: History and Analysis". Salt's scholarship goes into a meticulous analysis of film technologies as it pertains to camera movement, and stylistic development. This subject is interesting as it is a guidebook for filmmakers and film-related tech savants to properly use film technologies to manufacture specific effects in their movies. Therefore, scholars interested in film construction or in technology as a whole would benefit from Salt's scholarship. However, there are shortcomings to Salt's book. Despite a methodical coverage of film technologies, Salt only investigates these technologies as they pertain to American and/or European cinema. It can be asserted that during the time period this scholarship was written in, other global cinemas such as Asian cinema did not have much of an impact for scholars like Salt to include in their analysis, but these cinemas still existed. What is missing in this literature is thus a global perspective on the use of film technologies. Therefore, this paper posits that the Korean film industry expands on the global understanding of the dolly as a film technology by adopting the tracking shot as a template to achieving glocalization.

Korea in Action: Re-opening the *Kimchi* Refrigerator

Nataleya Slade

Abstract

This paper looks to evaluate the economic and social context in which the kimchi refrigerator emerged as a response to the '*kimchi* problem', as well as the adaptations made to the foreign imported refrigerator that then led to the uniquely Korean *kimchi* refrigerator. By exploring why fermentation of *kimchi* became a problem and the research to solve it that led to the eventual creation of the *kimchi* refrigerator, we can generate an image of not only the social construction of technology and technological need, but also attitudes toward technology. This problem will then be wrapped up by evaluating the 'Koreaness' of *kimchi* refrigeration, not solely based on *kimchi* making but on the reconfiguration of the refrigerator to fit the society it exists within. After establishing the kimchi refrigerator as Korean technology, this paper aims to uncover the historical situation in which the original *kimchi* fridges failed and what differed a decade later to cause the larger success and diffusion of the *kimchi* refrigerator, situating the *kimchi* refrigerator at the crossroad of society and technology. By doing this, this paper plans to fill in a gap within the larger research on *kimchi* refrigrator and even on what Korean technology is, that evaluates not only the technological and research oriented aspects, but also societal situations that shape technology that isn't Korean into something that can be considered Korean.

Introduction

In the average South Korean home, there is one appliance that will nearly always be present; the *kimchi* refrigerator. Used to store and ferment *kimchi*, keep fruits and vegetables fresher for longer and prevent food waste from spoiling before it can be tossed, this refrigerator has found use outside of its primary purpose—i.e., storing and fermenting *kimchi*. Born from the technology of the imported refrigerator, there then arises the question of social construction of technology and whether or not this product can be considered Korean technology. In the growing field of Korean technology, what makes a technology Korean is the most important consideration. If asked to name Korean technology or science, most people would list off advancements made by conglomerates such as KIA Automobiles and Samsung—modern companies that make their own products and are wholly Korean in origin. Thus, that makes what they produce Korean, of course. But what about the refrigerator? Considering it was imported in the late 1900s, we can conclude that it is a foreign technology[1]. Then what of the kimchi refrigerator? Deviated from imported refrigerator technology, what then makes this invention uniquely Korean is a question frequently overlooked and oversimplified to be because of the fact that it was made to solve a problem for product that is uniquely Korean. The '*kimchi* problem', which I define as the unique issue of fermenting *kimchi* in South Korea in the late 1900's, was the basis for research from the 1950's onward, ultimately resulting in a new technology to solve it. Scholarship has primarily strayed from technology that is considered to be obviously Korean. However, the *kimchi* refrigerator is Korean for many more reasons than just being made as a response to the '*kimchi* problem'.

There is merit in evaluating a product's ability to be Korean technology in terms of adaptations that follow society and usage; these tell us a lot about how the product actually became to be or not be widely used. Unlike many other scholars in the field, I look into the interesting situation that arises when looking at the technology of the *kimchi* refrigerator and the society within with it emerged. Despite the first kimchi refrigerator, the GR-063 made by GoldStar in 1984, being the 'needed solution' to the 'kimchi problem', it was not much of a success. Even with this failure, research didn't stop—Samsung even patented the kimchi

---

[1] Choi, Hyungsub. [Han'guk T'ek'ŭno K'ŏlch'ŏ Yŏndaegi] (18), "Kimch'i Naengjanggonŭn 'Han'gukhyŏng' T'ek'ŭnolloji in'ga?", weekly.khan.co.kr. *Chugan Kyŏng'hyang*, issue 1775, May 3, 2016. https://weekly.khan.co.kr/khnm.html?mode=view&artid=201605031403391&code=116.

refrigeration process in 1989, a futile attempt to keep the technology to themselves. Futile primarily because in 1995 the *Winia Dimch'ae* Kimchi Refrigerator, made by Mando, was born—a refrigerator that, to this day, is more widely known as the first kimchi refrigerator than the GR-063. What prohibited the early solution from being success and what attributed to the *Dimch'ae's* success is what this paper explores, setting the reason within both the technical and socio-economical spheres. By looking wholistically at the kimchi refrigerator's timeline, both as a technology and buyable product, this paper then argues that there was not enough significant change in technology from the GR-063 to the *Dimch'ae* to account for such a stark contrast in success. Therefore, I provide evidence that suggests and points to the success not being related to the technology itself, but instead to the socio-economic situation in which it emerged.

My primary argument, then, is that the *kimchi* refrigerator is a Korean technology that was created to solve the unique '*kimchi* problem' and I evaluate the journey of the technology's successes and failures in terms of socio-economic factors. This will open up scholarship on the topic of the *kimchi* refrigerator, especially regarding the 'Koreanness' of the product, and, for the larger field, fill a gap in scholarship. The *Kimchi* refrigerator, despite being a technology that has existed for over forty years, has scarcely been considered outside the technological and scientific aspects, which limits the scholarships ability to accurately capture the image of the *kimchi* refrigerator in society. Not only that, the scholarship has remained silent regarding the decade of 'stagnation' (i.e. minimal improvement in the technology of *kimchi* refrigerators). I start my evaluation of the *kimchi* refrigerator at the beginning of this period, and end at the first successful *kimchi* refrigerator, examining the social construction of technology through this 'stagnation'. By addressing the lacunae in scholarship, I refine the imaginary of Korean technology and how the *kimchi* refrigerator fits within it.

What is the *'kimchi'* problem?

In the 1970's, following the Second Five-Year Economic Plan (1967-71), South Korea began to build and bulk up their industry. In the 1970's alone, there was an increase urbanization numbers, moving people from the heavily populated rural areas to the urban ones in search of work, cheaper living, and for education[2] .

---

[2] Sung, Ho Ko. "Urban Growth in South Korea, 1970-1980: An Application of a Human Ecological Perspective". Korea Journal of Population and Development 23, no. 1 (July 1994)

What are now South Korea's metropolitan areas were just up and coming urban centers. These urban people also needed to eat *kimchi*—but they were no longer able to make it the way it was made throughout history.

Kimchi comes in a wide variety and each variety differs according to region and localization of the fermentation process. For example, in the Kyŏnggi Province, *kimchi* is characterized by lots of salted fish, called *jeotgal*, in the sauce base. However, while the flavor may differ, *kimchi* is typically made the same way; after being tucked away in an *onngi*, an earthenware container, the *kimchi* is then placed into a hole in ground and kept there for the fermentation process and also as a form of storage. Because *kimchi* is fermented using bacteria, if not stored properly these bacteria multiply too fast and both taste and longevity are affected.[3] *Kimchi's* unique flavor comes from these germs. Regular refrigerators, which would have been more common in urban areas than rural, cannot properly recreate the temperature that *kimchi* usually sits at in ground. The average refrigerator seeks just to keep food cool, whereas the ground is cold to the point of freezing.[4] Therefore, early on urban areas run into the issue of *kimchi's* taste and texture suffering if it is not stored and fermented in the ground. Thus, the *kimchi* problem emerges and in the absence of slowing industrialization, research frantically seeks to find an answer.

We can buy *kimchi* at the store whenever we want to, but in the 1970's, at a time when fridges weren't even used widespread throughout Korea, this was not even an option for the most well off. The first method that researchers try is wholesale *kimchi* products, but they run into several problems in their research. The first issue they run into is the extreme difficulty in making *kimchi* uniformly—modern research now has the knowledge of starter cultures that can help curb this issue, but in the 1970's and 80's, this research was wholly absent.[5] Another issue they run across is the standardization of *kimchi*. Mentioned in the prior paragraph, *kimchi* is extremely variable and can even be different from family to family, let alone region to region. To standardize *kimchi*, companies have to decide on what the most basic, 'true' *kimchi* flavor is. Even today, many people still make their *kimchi* from scratch during the *kimchi* season, customizing their *kimchi* to taste. Adding on to this, recent research suggests that the flavor achieved in the *onngi*,

---

[3] Jung, et. al. "Kimchi Microflora". Appl Microbiol Biotechnol, 2014; 1-2, DOI 10.1007/s00253-014-5513-1

[4] Hong, Sangsun. "Onggi ŏksa yŏtpogi" in Sum Swinŭn Tojagi Onggi: Chayŏnŭl Tamgo Salmi Mudŏnanŭn Iyagi (2010), 150-169.

[5] Jung, "Kimchi Microflora", 1-2.

despite the advanced *kimchi* refrigerators that exist today, tastes better, suggesting that kimchi refrigeration technology itself is not the only issue regarding taste.[6] The last reason that wholesale of *kimchi* was a failure during this period is that industrialization and home technology were extremely new to the Korean population—many people were not ready to give up on traditional methods of fermentation and many believe, like the above research also suggests, that *onngi* made *kimchi* is superior.

Due to such a wide variety of cultural aspects regarding *kimchi*, it was much simpler to provide people instead with something they can use to continue to make *kimchi* themselves. And because there was extensive research done on the fermentation of *kimchi*, both in measuring the temperature and the fermentation levels, all that was left to create a technology that would recreate the traditional process. And therefore the first *kimchi* refrigerator was born.

Is The Kimchi Refrigerator a 'Korean' Technology?

So then the question remains, is the *kimchi* refrigerator, South Korea's answer to the essential '*kimchi* problem, Korean technology? I argue that yes, it is. However, my main argument for this will rest outside the consideration of the *kimchi* refrigerator as a substitution for fermenting *kimchi*. *Kimchi* is quintessentially Korean—there has been various dispute of whether or not *kimchi* is Korean over the last few years, but as of late, resolute understanding that it is, in fact, Korean has settled.[7] And not just Korean, but uniquely Korean. The long running argument between South Korea and China over the novelty of *kimchi* primarily stems the translation of all salted, fermented foods as *kimchi*, rather than as 'salted, fermented vegetables'. Several scholars have even come out, tracing *kimchi* all the way back to the *Koryo* period and disproving the claims that red pepper did not exist in Korea prior to the Imjin War.[8] Therefore, if *kimchi* is Korean, then the '*kimchi* problem' is uniquely Korean and thus the *kimchi* refrigerator is also Korean.

---

[6] Jeong, et. al. "Increased quality and functionality of kimchi when fermented in Korean earthenware (onngi)", International Journal of Food Science and Technology (46), 2011.

[7] Kim, Youmi and Mike Ives. "Is China Laying Claim to Kimchi too? Some South Koreans Think So." New York Times, December 10, 2020, https://www.nytimes.com/2020/12/01/world/asia/south-korea-china-kimchi-paocai.html

[8] Jang, et. al. "Discussion on the origin of kimchi, representative of Korean unique fermented vegetables", *Journal of Ethnic Foods*, September 2015; 127.

But the *kimchi* refrigerator is Korean for more than just being made to store and facilitate fermentation processes. In adapting the *kimchi* refrigerators build, aesthetic, and interface, there have been careful considerations of who is using the product, what the product can be used for, and much fine tuning to make it sellable to the Korean people. By fine tuning the product to the Korean people and through usage expansion within the Korean populace, the *kimchi* refrigerator has made its place in Korean society much more secure.

The first *kimchi* refrigerator was advertised to only able to handle roughly 18kg, which was only considered to be enough for a 5-person family to eat ten single person servings of *kimchi*.[9] This size was much too small to hold the amount of *kimchi* made during *kimchi* season—which is typically a year or at least half a year's worth of *kimchi* and definitely more than 18kg. Because of its small size, the first *kimchi* refrigerators were partially unable to become huge successes, though the ones that did succeed were not much larger. Nowadays, people can buy *kimchi* refrigerators the size of their actual fridge. As the market flooded with more *kimchi* refrigerators, consumers had options and their options then influenced what adaptions were made to later refrigerators. Not only that, the first *kimchi* refrigerators only had temperature options and these options had to be monitored and adjusted according to the fermentation process by the consumer themselves.[10] Later *kimchi* refrigerators introduced significantly more buttons and processes— but recent research has been influencing a recent trend toward simpler and elder friendly *kimchi* refrigerators.[11] [12] Adjusting to South Korea's large elder population in terms of technology, especially considering they would be the main consumers of it, demonstrates that the technology does not just exist to simply do the work of fermenting *kimchi*, but is also constructed socially by the society in which it exists.

Recent research has examine the composition of the *kimchi* refrigerator and how this build hinders its usability among the target consumer population (older women). The first *kimchi* refrigerators were all top-open refrigerators, meaning

---

[9] Kŭmsŏngsa, "Kungnae Ch'oech'o Kŭmsŏng Kimch'inaengjanggo T'ansaeng", *Chosun Ilbo*, 1984.

[10] Kŭmsŏngsa, "Kungnae Ch'oech'o Kŭmsŏng Kimch'inaengjanggo T'ansaeng", 1984.

[11] Park, et. al. "Chunggoryŏng Chuburŭl Koryŏhan Kimch'inaengjanggo Cheŏp'anŭi Sayongja Int'ŏp'eisŭ Tijain [User Interface Design of the Control Panel of Kimchi Refrigerator for the Older Women]", *Journal of the Ergonomics Society of Korea*, vol. 28, no. 3, August 2009, pp. 27-31.

[12] Lee, et. al. "Mullijŏk Sayongja Int'ŏp'eisŭ Ch'ŭngmyŏnesŏ Kimch'inaengjanggoŭi Sayongja Manjokto Chosa [Survey of Customer Satisfaction of Kimchi Refrigerators with Focus on Physical User Interfaces]", *Journal of the Ergonomics Society of Korea*, vol. 26, no. 4, 2007, pp. 113-120.

they had a lid that opened and everything was placed inside the refrigerator stacked on top of each other. This posed great of difficulty for older women especially, who were typically the main ones making and dealing with the *kimchi* of a household. These older women, though younger women did the same, reported extreme levels of discomfort using the refrigerator because they had to bend at the waist and lift heavy products.[13] We can assume these trends existed for early *kimchi* refrigerators as well—there was little surveying done regarding usage of the product because it wasn't until 1994 that the *kimchi* refrigerator even began to appear in many homes. The first *kimchi* refrigerators were largely top-open models but later in the 1990's that drawer models even emerged in a variety of forms—cabinet inserts and freestanding were the most popular. The *kimchi* refrigerator's build has accommodated room for other, non-fermented foods since conception as well. The first *kimchi* refrigerator had a hanging basket that rested above the space for *kimchi* containers, though it wasn't large enough to be a stacking model. Most likely because the *kimchi* refrigerator needed to be sold figuratively to the populace, there was advertisement of its variety of uses early on, such as being used to store vegetables for longer and keep vegetables such as lettuce and cucumber crispier.[14] This may even be able to account for why the models took a turn and started to look more like refrigerators—because of their high price, they most likely needed to be marketed with more than one use and as a technology that would transform more than just their *kimchi* making.

These adjustments and advancements that the *kimchi* refrigerator has made since inception, are then, more indicative of the Korean society and the interaction between them and the technology. What makes technology Korean is then more than just making products, especially when the technology that goes into it is not completely novel. The *kimchi* refrigerator is only one example of a technology, that while having evolved from imported technology, it has now taken on a new form. But technology is also constructed through society's use of it. And therefore, to get a complete view of *how* a technology is Korean, it should be evaluated from all angles. Stopping evaluation of the koreanness of the *kimchi* refrigerator at being used for *kimchi* is only grazing the surface of the technology's significance and use in the Korean society and by demonstrating how the changes made reflect the Korean society at large, I argue for a deeper and more in depth approach to evaluating technology and societies.

---

[13] Lee, "Mullijŏk Sayongja Int'ŏp'eisŭ...". 117

[14] Kŭmsŏngsa, "Kungnae Ch'oech'o Kŭmsŏng Kimch'inaengjanggo T'ansaeng", 1984.

The World's First Kimchi Refrigerator

So where does the story of the *kimchi* refrigerator begin? If you ask anyone in Korea, at least before 2015, they would have told you that the 1994 *Dimch'ae* was the first *kimchi* refrigerator. But truthfully, the story begins before that, in 1984 with GoldStar's GR-063.

GoldStar's 1984 GR-063

Resources regarding the first kimchi refrigerator models is very scarce—they are all typically grouped together under technology type, such as top-open, free standing, direct cooling, etc. and not evaluated on an individual, model basis. On top of that, the GR-063 was given very little attention for a long time, so there are few surviving models to even look at. Despite that, there are some things that we can learn about this model from the original ad that it was released in and from research on how the kimchi refrigerator was made from the technology used in the imported refrigerators.

The GR-063, sitting at 45 liters, was made of stainless steel inside with a plastic finish on the outside. These first models were white bodied with a clear green lid that opened on both sides for easy access to the inside. The model also came with a basket for fruits and vegetables and the advertisement specifically mentioned giving away a set of plastic containers (4) with purchases.[15] Outside of these specifics, not much else is known regarding the GR-063. While not the most sleek and sophisticated model, it did the job and was the solution to the 'kimchi problem'. At least, it was marketed that way. The ad for the GR-063 depicts who they expect their target to be (housewives) and explains what the company believes to be the most important things that the *kimchi* refrigerator can do (hold *kimchi* and other fresh fruits and vegetables). This reflects scholarship that states that households at that time were not utilizing the refrigerator, let alone a *kimchi* fridge, because they grocery shopped more frequently and bought and ate food within the same day.[16]

Despite the GR-063 being a clear solution to the 'kimchi problem', a problem that even the Korean Atomic Energy Institute aided in research to solve, it was a complete failure.[17] The product adequately solved the problem according to

---

15 Kŭmsŏngsa, "Kungnae Ch'oech'o Kŭmsŏng Kimch'inaengjanggo T'ansaeng", 1984.

16 "Kimch'i Naengjanggonŭn 'Han'gukhyŏng' T'ek'ŭnolloji in'ga?", 2016.

17 Choi, "Kimch'i Naengjanggo'nŭn 'Han'gukhyŏng' T'ek'ŭnolloji in'ga?", 2016.

available technology, but it was not picked up by consumers at the expected rate. This is where the concept of society constructed technology and the *kimchi* refrigerator's successes and failures comes into play.

Timing of the GR-063

To evaluate a technology, there has to be consideration of the socio-economic situation in which it arose, as well as the cultural attitude towards the product itself, which influences whether or not it is successful. For the case of South Korea, economically it was set up for failure after the Korean War. Despite US financial support, the fact of the matter was that South Korea lacked the industry to compete in a global economy, let alone 'develop' their own nation to global standards. Korea as a whole developed significantly during the colonial period, albeit to support Japan, but because of this, most of their industry was concentrated towards the Korean boundary to Japan's Manchurian colony, and the southern half was left to take care of the agriculture. After the split and South Korea's implementation of a national government, there were significant movements to combat this, such as the series of Five-Year Plans. This was not only to increase urbanization in South Korea, but also to increase population in metropolitan areas and develop the nation according to global standards. We can consider this as part of the reason why South Korea is considered one of the four 'tigers of the East'.[18]

If we look toward Urbanization in the 1960's in South Korea happened at an accelerated rate. Typical of developing countries, which South Korea was at the time, South Korea grew nearly exponentially. Much of the urbanization during the 60's was concentrated in Seoul, which had gained nearly two-thirds of the net urban migrants. Naturally, outside of Seoul, there was significant movement out of the rural areas and into both cities and their surrounding urban areas. Much of this was because of the emergence of industry, which was a main focus of the First Five-Year Plan (1962-66), that brought rural workers to the cities in order to fill the positions that these industries needed. Urbanization was significant in the 1960's but slowed in Seoul in the following decade, where there was instead a large influx of people into the surrounding urban areas. Most of the people moving to yhese urban areas were not areas that were exactly yearning for a *kimchi* solution—some of them could still burying their *onngi* in their yards since apartments were concentrated in the metropolitan areas, not the urban ones. By

---

[18] Seth, Michael, *A Concise History of Korea* (Rowman & Littlefield, 2016), 2 ed.

the end of the 1970's, urbanization into Seoul had halved and consistently stayed at those numbers well into the 1980's. [19] What this means in terms of the *kimchi* refrigerator, exactly, is that there was not enough need for it—most of people who would've needed this product were still concentrated in the rural countryside and the recipients of the labor that goes into *kimchi* making were concentrated in the cities and less so in the urban areas. Additionally, the GR-063 *kimchi* refrigerator was marketed for families, not for the single individual, which was not the primary market in Seoul at that time. [20] [21] The majority of the Seoul city population, especially during the 1980's, was comprised of students and young adult men and women, not older women who did much of the *kimchi* making until recent decades.

Urbanization is only half the story of the situation in South Korea at the time. The economic situation in South Korea in the 1980's was not one that was able to support new technology. At the turn of the decade, South Korea had entered a recession and had climbing rates of unemployment.[22] The current leadership of the time, Chun Doo Hwan, as a response to this enacted the Fifth Five-Year Plan (1982-86) and fought to battle inflation and bring economic recovery exclusively for the first two years.[23] This Fifth Five-Year Economic Plan would be important in giving support to technology-intensive industries, such home technology, including the *kimchi* refrigerator. By the 1980's, *kimchi* research had been going on for over thirty years but no technology to rectify it had come forth. Timing-wise, the *kimchi* refrigerator came out right as there was a push for more in-home technological advancement, exactly what the government was hoping for. However, the *kimchi* fridge itself was probably not the best technology to entice consumer consumption of technology during the 1980's, hence its large failure. Based on the economic situation at the time, there was most likely not a large enough customer base that could even afford the product when it was released.

According to this, the situation during the 1980's was clearly lacking in both economic ability and also need, both of which are basic functions of economics and create the movement of the market. Dually, if the need of the product is not high enough, there usually isn't enough energy put into research, however, since *kimchi* was so central to independent national thought, it was pursued tirelessly and

---

[19] Savada, et. al., *South Korea, A Country Study* (Library of Congress, 1994), 145.

[20] *IBID.*

[21] Kŭmsŏngsa, "Kungnae Ch'oech'o Kŭmsŏng Kimch'inaengjanggo T'ansaeng", 1984.

[22] Haggard, et. al., *Macroeconomic Policy and Adjustment in Korea, 1970-1990* (Harvard University Press, 1994), 82-3

[23] Savada, et. al., South Korea, A Country Study.

as soon as the technology was available, it was released. But if there is no one who can afford the product or who has a need for it over traditional methods, or even over the Korean refrigerator, then it is pretty clearly doomed to not do well. Sometimes the economic situation can be overcome—that is when cultural thought and ideas of perceived importance emerge strongly alongside the product. However, the 80's were marked by intense political rift and student protest, where a product endorsed by government plans and support may not have been well received. Additionally, at this time, many Koreans still bought their fruits and vegetables at markets often, meaning they had no need for a fridge of any kind. Many older people, who do much of the *kimchi* making, were not yet ready to give up on traditional methods. Thus, it is almost a given that the *kimchi* refrigerator fail the first time around. [24]

The First Successful *Kimchi* Refrigerator, the *Winia Dimch'ae* (1994)

After the nearly humiliating failure of the first *kimchi* refrigerator, and the subsequent ones released by companies like Samsung, Daewoo, etc., it was almost a surprise when the *kimchi* refrigerator market was revitalized in 1994. Not only was it revitalized, but it was a large success and since that point in history purchases of the *kimchi* refrigerator have only gone up every year. What makes the *Winia Dimch'ae* a success is then the question—was it the technology itself, the socio-economic situation or something else completely? While the technology of course differed from its counterpart ten years prior, the difference was not large enough to account for such a huge success. Instead of looking to technology, looking towards the socio-economic situation in which the *Winia Dimch'ae* was born into, shows that it was more conducive to the technology and the climate was one in which the technology could become a success.

Mando's Winia Dimch'ae (1994)—The 'First' Kimchi Refrigerator

Similarly to the GR-063, next to nothing is known about the exacts of the CFR-052E, better known as the *Winia Dimch'ae*. Even a search into newspaper archives doesn't pull up much from the year of conception (1994), hinting at a different mode of media being used to advertise the product. It also demonstrates the lack

---

[24] Choi, "Kimch'i Naengjanggo'nŭn 'Han'gukhyŏng' T'ek'ŭnolloji in'ga?", 2016.

of media attention paid to it within the first year, so there is no obvious ad or commercial that can be evaluated to find the specifics of this fridge. It can be assumed that it was slightly bigger than the GR-063, was also a stacking and top-opening model, and used direct cooling based on photos. It is rumored on news sites that the *Winia Dimch'ae* had more control options in terms of *kimchi* fermentation, but without a physical model to view, it is hard to confirm that information.[25] Interestingly, the *Winia* brand that created the *Dimch'ae* refrigerator models was a subset of Mando, an air conditioning engineering company, rather than an appliance company like GoldStar was. The make and build of the *Dimch'ae* model follows the GR-063 closely—the green and white plastic exterior and the stainless steel interior would make them identical if the *Dimch'ae* wasn't slightly taller than the GR-063. So, technology wise, they haven't been shown in research or released advertisements to be significantly different from each other. If anything, the *Dimch'ae* used the GR-063 as a model and the name, *Dimch'ae* also insinuates a return to the past with *kimchi* refrigeration. The main difference would be in the wider range of fermentation options with the *Dimch'ae*—while the GR-063 had only around a 7 degree range, the *Dimch'ae's* range was a bit larger. So if the technologies were not differently enough to constitute one over the other, why then was the *Dimch'ae* such a favorite in 1994 and the GR-063 practically ignored in 1984? Moving away from technology and instead looking at society differences between the *Dimch'ae* and the GR-063 can tell the story from the angle of the consumers and their socio-economic stance.

South Korea and the 1990's—home of Dimch'ae

The socio-economic climate of the 1990's was radically different than that of its '80's counterpart. While the early '80's was rife with economic and political instability, the economic situation of the 1990's was emerging strong, primarily because of the five-year programs that led up to it and the financial liberalization that was occurring as a result. The political climate had begun to stabilize during this time as well, as student movements had died out with reforms. Also during this time is the expansion of 'apartment living' in cities and urban areas, which

---

[25] Lee, Sang-hoon, "Kimch'i Naengjanggoŭi 'Wŏnjo' Ŏdi'in Chul Asinayo?", *IT Chosun*, April 24, 2015.

would then expand the market for the *kimchi* refrigerator significantly as people outside of these two areas had low to no need for it.[26]

Economically, the 1990's was demonstrating the fruits of the labor of all the previous Five-Year Plans, with industry flourishing and home technological companies being able to import technology from abroad to reverse engineer them into Korean products. What set the 90's up for success was partly the Sixth Five-Year Economic Plan (1987-91). With this plan, the government phased out specific economic help and also worked to uplift small and medium sized businesses which created more jobs and aided in more relocation. The government also accelerated import liberation, which was part of the economic liberation movement that began in the late 1980's. This would make at home products more popular, as the imported products began to rise in price. Additionally, the *chaebol* companies that had long received funds from the government were now independent and the government could spend this money elsewhere, freeing the economy.[27]

Economic liberation, a form of policy making that South Korea is characterized during this period, was a mode of economic policy that sought to make importation and exportation generally free-flowing, as well as liberate the economy from underneath the state's thumb. Loan amounts increased and the housing market began to move towards the institution of 'key money', better known as South Korea's deposit system for housing. The credit system expanded drastically—credit cards and loans were the easiest to obtain than they've ever been, while simultaneously being the largest they've ever been. All in all there was significantly more money in the larger market and in people's pockets which made the *kimchi* refrigerator a more plausible buy than before.[28]

Following this change closely was also the apartment boom. Apartment living in the 1980's was sparsely practiced and apartments were generally concentrated in the Seoul Metropolis. This boom happened as a direct result of the Rho regime's "Two Million Housing Units Construction Plan", which was enacted to solve the drastic homelessness and unaffordable housing problem that was running throughout South Korea since the 1970's.[29] While inefficient to solve the homeless

---

[26] Park, Bae-Gyoon, "Where Do Tigers Sleep at Night? The State's Role in Housing Policy in South Korea and Singapore", *Economic Geography*, Vol. 74, No. 3, July 1998, 272-288.

[27] Savada, et. al., *South Korea, A Country Study*, 144-49.

[28] *IBID.*

[29] Park, "Where Do Tigers Sleep at Night?", 272-288.

issue in South Korea, it did provide the *kimchi* refrigerator with a larger market—now over two million people had need of a *kimchi* refrigerator and could most likely afford it due to expanded credit and loan ability. While this practice was bad for the economy in the long run—the IMF crisis of 1997 dubbed Korea's worst depression in history. Ignoring the later consequences of such a rapid expansion of housing and opening of importation and economy, these were extremely conducive economic expansion, which allowed the *kimchi* refrigerator to thrive like it hadn't been able to a decade prior.

Conclusion

Socially Constructed Technology

The *kimchi* refrigerator is thus a technology that is less about its advancements and specifications and more about the timing of its introduction into society. Because the first *kimchi* refrigerator and the first successful *kimchi* refrigerator were extremely similar, even down to the color of their lid and exterior, what differentiated their success has to be something outside the realm of technological advancement. A cultural and socio-economic approach to the issue explains this, then. And this is not just limited to the *kimchi* refrigerator—consideration of what makes a technology Korean is not just limited to its reason for conception or what it's perceived to be used for. Any history of technology must look beyond the product and further into the society that it is being introduced into. What makes a product a success or a failure? This question and questions like it are not limited to technological and scientific considerations—I would argue, even, that when research fails to look beyond products and into the society within which the product was born, it fails to evaluate technology properly at all.

So, then, the *kimchi* refrigerator is Korean technology that arose from the Korean specific '*kimchi* problem' and then saw a series of successes and failures based on the period within which it emerged in a Korean society. What determines a technology to be Korean, if that sub-category can exist, involves more than just being for a Korean product. The *kimchi* refrigerator is Korean because it's adaptions, successes, failures and are a reflection of its use and role in Korean society—'Koreaness' is not just intended use but, arguably, is more about actual use. And the *kimchi* refrigerator, a technology that has long been overlooked, brings to light an interesting story regarding what makes technology Korean and how technology and society work together to determine the fate of technology. After evaluating the socio-economic factors of South Korea during the time of the *kimchi* refrigerators introduction, the blurry image of society and technology's relationship begins to sharpen. Research has ignored the way that the relationship between science and technology has emerged in household products, and the *kimchi* refrigerator has suffered the most. Hopefully research can, in the future, recognize the complicated nature of the relationship that national technology portrays of society and science. Alas, the *kimchi* refrigerator's story does not end here, but at least the lid has been opened.

Laundry Machines: From Gendered Labor to Industrialization

Paulina Joo

Abstract

"The washing machine changed the world more than the internet," Ha-Joon-Chang, a Cambridge University economist, remarked. Housework automation goes beyond enhancing labor efficiency, but Korean researchers have failed to comprehend this broader component of housework mechanization. Based on the foregoing understanding of the problem, the following paper will examine the socioeconomic context that underlies the introduction and diffusion of washing machines in Korea. In addition, we will examine the alleged contribution of washing machines in structuring domestic work in Korea. Korea has a long and unique tradition of wearing white clothes, which necessitated washing clothes more regularly and so formed a cultural framework around it. To analyze the introduction of washing machines, we will focus on Kumsung's modifications in marketing strategies utilized to promote the "Swan Laundry Machine" in order to efficiently penetrate the new market. The spread of washing machines during the rapid industrialization of Korea resulted in higher living standards and wages, as well as changes in women's social status. In this paper, I'll use the Cowan paradox framework to examine how the introduction of laundry machines influenced Korean households' domestic lives.

Introduction

Industrialization of housework

As industrialization progressed in the 1960s, various home devices such as laundry machines, refrigerators, and vacuum machines were introduced into Korea. As these devices spread, women's roles and domestic life underwent changes. The transformation can be framed into two ways: industrialization of housework and mechanization of housework. Here, housework refers to a set of physical tasks such as cooking, cleaning, laundry, and taking care of household members. The term mechanization of housework limits the influence within the household, whereas industrialization of domestic labor extends its impact to the society. This paper aims to explore the socioeconomic context that underlies the introduction and diffusion of washing machines in Korea.

Korean scholars have previously examined the mechanization of housework. However, they failed to capture the socio-economic aspect of this movement.[1] Research on the history of science and technology deals with the transition of industrial devices, but the subject of research in Korea was manufacturers. Korea's first "Swan Laundry Machine" by Kumsung was also listed as a cultural asset, but it was registered for the purpose of protecting cultural properties rather than examining the historic background and the diffusion of the machine.[2]

Korea, being one of the leading players in the home appliance industry, with a market revenue of 2.1 billion won, many papers focused on the technological breakthroughs and its recent achievements. However, they failed to investigate the historical background behind the achievements and the influence it had on Korea's domestic environment. In awareness of this problem, this study aims to encapsulate the historic background behind the introduction of washing machines, their diffusion process, and their contribution to reshaping domestic labor in South Korea.

Among the variety of household services, this study focuses on laundry since housewives spent 2 hours on average doing laundry and was considered one of most tedious work. After the introduction of washing machines, housewives saved

---

[1] Lee, Ki Young. "The mechanization of Housework: Focused on Diffusion Process and influencing Factors". Kajŏnggwa Salmŭi Chil Yŏn'gu (2002): 70-80.

[2] *IBID.*

80% of their time spent on doing laundry, allowing themselves to spend more time on other activities such as leisure, childcare, and economic activities.[3]

The root of "The People of White Clothes"

White clothing is a symbol of ethnicity for Korea and represents cleanliness as well as class. Since ancient times, Korea has been called "The People of White Clothes," and it is evident that Korea has long liked to wear white clothes in historical records. *Samgukji* and *Wiji-dungeon* recorded that "Buui revered white and wore white clothes widely," and "all the clothes of those who bent down in the green fields were white." The ruling class discriminated against ordinary people in white by wearing colorful clothes. In the Three Kingdoms period, clothes with colorful patterns and vivid hues were mainly imported from the Chinese Dynasty, making them unaffordable to most commoners. For this reason, most people wore white clothes except for the ruling class. For that reason, *"paeksŏng"*, which indicates commoners during the Chosŏn dynasty, originated from the word *"paekŭi"*, meaning white clothes.

Before, commoners wore white clothes due to social restrictions; however, even after eliminating the status system, some still wore white clothes due to the lack of dyeing materials and techniques. The Japanese colonial period changed white clothes into a symbol of anti-Japanese sentiment, and people began to identify themselves as "The People of White Clothes." Despite the inefficient color that increases the frequency of laundry, the preference for white clothes has decreased only after liberation.

Joy and sorrow of laundry

Korea has a unique history of being tied with white clothes; women spent a lot of time and effort washing white clothes where stains were most visible. As a result, numerous cleaning methods arose spontaneously throughout Korea. In the past, Korea has used hand washing, along with unique washing methods such as tapping clothes to wash ramie and boiling washing to remove dark stains from white clothes. Besides the technical developments, laundry was considered a social activity.

---

[3] Mun, Hye Gyŏng. "set'akpangbŏbŭi pyŏnch'ŏn'gwa set'akki paldare kwanhan yŏn'gu." (1997): 1-70.

Doing laundry was considered leisure activity during the Chosŏn dynasty; homemakers sat by streams or rivers, had casual conversations with neighbors, recounted their daily lives, and sung to the sound of bats while doing their laundry. Kim Hong-do, a folk artist from the Joseon Dynasty, also shows this in his works. Laundry was a subject that was common in Joseon's artworks.

Furthermore, the washing site was mentioned several times in the lyrics of "Songs of Living in a Family," a labor song that women sang together while doing laundry, which was documented in the study of narrative folk songs. Some explained that this was the only time when females were freed from their homes to meet their friends under the pretext of doing laundry. According to Confucian belief, it was held that men's and women's principles could never be mixed. Women's and men's activities were clearly separated by "in-house" and "out-of-home," and women's living areas were strictly separated from men's.

The practice of doing laundry together was commonly seen until the 1960s. Laundry that had previously been done in a shared area was shifted to a highly private venue due to the expansion of water and sewerage services in the 1960s. Homemakers had to do the same burdensome task alone in their homes. Laundry was no longer a "social activity" and was categorized as "work." Due to a shift in perception on laundry, the demand for mechanization of the laundry process surged among housewives and laundry machines started to appear in Korean households in the 1970s.

Introduction of washing machines

Background

On top of laundry becoming mundane daily work, the frequency of laundry increased due to the popularity in fashion and introduction of clothes made out of textiles that needed to be handled with extra caution. With dyes becoming easier to access, demand for white clothes declined, and vivid colored clothes gained popularity throughout Korea. Nonetheless, as a result of the increased exposure to fashion, many materials requiring caution were imported into Korea, resulting in a rise in the frequency and quantity of laundering. Homemakers were trapped in a monotonous routine at home, washing and ironing loads of laundry. The development of washing machines was stalled by technological limitations even though demand for mechanization of the laundry process skyrocketed.

Following the 1960s, the electronic industry around home appliances began to grow in earnest with economic development.   Contrary to common wisdom, the development of laundry machines in South Korea was initiated not by a drive to reduce the burden of domestic labor but by to drive the South Korean economy. In Korea, home appliance supply was closely related to the projected size of the industry and the company's technical capabilities, with producers' efficiency prioritized over consumers' efficiency.[4] This aspect was well represented in the introduction of washing machines to households.

According to a 1975 survey, 30 percent of homemakers wanted to buy washing machines, and 7 percent preferred refrigerators.[5] The washing machine, which was more demanding for homemakers, was developed in 1969, four years after the refrigerator.[6]

Introduction of laundry machines to South Korea

In the 15th century, attempts to apply various hand movements to equipment began in the West. Efforts to mechanize laundry were first made in 1691 in England in a device that mimicked the back-and-forth motion of hands against uneven washing boards.[7] In 1851, James T. King invented the modern concept of the washing machine. King's washing machine replaced washing, rinsing, and drying with compressed air by repeated piston movements.[8] In 1908, American Alva John Fisher invented the first drum-type washer with an electric motor. Millet, a German manufacturer, recognized the industry's potential for expansion and began mass-producing drum-type washing machines with drying features. As a result of mass production, machine-related technology increased substantially, and retail prices of washing machines plummeted across Europe, making them more affordable. Despite minor design and feature changes, washing machines made in the United States, the United Kingdom, Germany, and Canada set the groundwork for modern designs like drum washers and barrel washers.

The Korean laundry machine market was initially created by importing products from Japan. Japan imported its first laundry machine model in 1921 and then

---

[4] Lee, Ki Young. "The mechanization of Housework: Focused on Diffusion Process and influencing Factors". Kajŏnggwa Salmŭi Chil Yŏn'gu (2002): 70-80.

[5] *IBID.*

[6] *IBID.*

[7] Mun, Hye Gyŏng. "set'akpangbŏbŭi pyŏnch'ŏn'gwa set'akki paldare kwanhan yŏn'gu." (1997): 1-70.

[8] *IBID.*

refined it to serve the lifestyle of East Asians better.[9] In the 1960s, Japan became a top player among East Asian countries by re-engineering technologies and simplifying operations.[10] In 1969, Kumsung introduced the WP-181 model in Korea under the name "Swan Laundry Machine" for a retail price of 53,000 won.[11] As Kumsang lacked the necessary technology to manufacture individual parts, Hitachi supplied the components and Kumsang was primarily involved in assembling them into the final product.[12] This manual aluminum model consisted of two separate containers: laundry containers and dehydration containers and could only accommodate 1.8 kilograms of laundry.[13] Initially, Kumsung thought to make 1,500 units; however, because of the unfamiliar public's slow adoption, Kumsung chose to limit production to 500 units.[14] Even though there were high expectations for demand, production was temporarily suspended after the first batch production of 195 units. Considering the starting salary is 20,000 won, the retail price of 53,000 won seemed too high to win the public's heart. On their debut, laundry machines were classed as luxury goods, and a 60 percent commodity tax was imposed. Imported parts made the product expensive and less appealing to the audience. Apart from the cost, Kumsung failed to change the perception that laundry is a woman's responsibility and that clothes can be destroyed if they are not cleaned by hand. Koreans who were used to wearing clothing made of fibers like cotton and hemp believed that using washing machines would degrade the shape and retention of their clothes.

Kumsung was not the only company that failed to enter the washer market. In the 1970s, Samsung Electronics jumped into the production of washing machines, and in 1973,   Kumho Electric and Wasung Electronic began production with a technology partnership with Japan's Toshiba and Sony. However, the production was soon discontinued due to a lack of recognition of need. In this paper, I have concentrated on Kumsung's "Swan Laundry Machine," which was

---

[9] Kim, Won-Jin, and Sung-Jin Chat. "Design Genealogy of Washing Machines and Their Mechanism." Journal of Korean Society of Design Science, 4, 15 (December 1, 2002): 370–78.

[10] *IBID.*

[11] Mun, Hye Gyŏng. "set'akpangbŏbŭi pyŏnch'ŏn'gwa set'akki paldare kwanhan yŏn'gu." (1997): 1–70.

[12] Kim, Won-Jin, and Sung-Jin Chat. "Design Genealogy of Washing Machines and Their Mechanism." Journal of Korean Society of Design Science, 4, 15 (December 1, 2002): 370–78.

[13] *IBID.*

[14] *IBID.*

the first Korean washing machine and underwent a series of marketing strategy modifications in order to successfully penetrate the new market.

Emphasizing need recognition

Homemakers spent 90% of their housework hours in the laundry room, proving that the laundry system needed to be instrumented. However, there was a lack of understanding of the need for laundry machines in the late 1960s. Many families, uninformed of the machine's capabilities, concluded that such technology was not worth spending two months' salary on. Kumsung pushed promotional efforts to appeal to new consumer demographics to address low sales due to a lack of customer understanding. This effort is evident in advertisements for Kumsung's "Swan Washing Machine" published in the Dong-A Ilbo in 1969, 1971, 1973, and 1974.

In 1969, Dongah Ilbo reported the first Korean washing machine. Under the headline "Washing Machine for One Minute," the article introduced a washing machine that will help many people during the summer with loaded laundry.[15] The article briefly covered the concepts and processes of washing machines, however the subject of time saving was only stated in the headline. Furthermore, the unrealistic headline caused an adverse effect on the audience by boldly stating that the machine will reduce the time spent on laundry from 2 hours to 1 minute.

Change in core message

While the previous newspaper ads focused on highlighting the features, Kumsung began a promotional campaign that appealed to emotions and the product's core benefits. In 1971, Kumsung published an ad with the headline, "laundry is a waste of time."[16] The article emphasized the core benefit of using the machine: it can save time invested in laundry and eliminate the need for a large laundry store. To create an emotional connection with homemakers, they also included lines that exhibited respect for homemakers who do laborious tasks, such as laundry, kitchen work, cleaning, and children's education. Additionally, "would you like to have a relaxed modern family?" was included as a call to action. This advertisement targeted various segments of women in

---

[15] Dongah Ilbo, 'Air Laundry Machine [공기세탁기]'. 1968 [Naver News Library]

[16]Dongah Ilbo, 'Laundry is a Waste of Time [빨래는 時間(시간)의 浪費(낭비) 입니다]'.1971 [Naver News Library]

diverse types of households, including newlyweds, apartment living families, married couples with two incomes, and large families. As most audiences were unfamiliar with washing machines, Kumsung chose advertising that targeted all women rather than focusing on homemakers in specific types of households. Since the early 1970s, the number of marriages has increased, and with the entrance of Western customs such as wedding hall culture and honeymoon customs, interest in home products to furnish new homes has spontaneously developed. The advertising strategy has undergone a change focusing on newlyweds who are favorable to a new culture and are making a new start.

Change in target audience

In 1973, Kumsung published an advertisement in Dongah Ilbo that delivered a message that washing machines would fulfill the dreams of newly married couples. There was a shift in the target audience and this time Kumsung was targeting both male and female audiences. With the rise of marriages since the early 1970s and the introduction of Western cultures such as wedding hall culture and honeymoon culture, attention has been drawn to home products to decorate new homes. Advertising strategy changed to target newlyweds who are disposed to a new culture and were preparing to make a new beginning. Compared with advertisements published in 1971, this ad narrowed down the target to new brides from all housewives and expanded its audience by appealing to newlywed grooms. After establishing the core benefits of washing machines in the minds of homemakers, the media specified its target audience as both female and male audiences of newly married couples.

In addition, Kumsung reframed the benefits of washing machines to suit the needs of newlyweds. Both 1971's and 1973's had emphasized time efficiency; however, there was a change in the perspective on the utilization of time saved. Previously, Kumsung emphasized that wives would be able to invest their time in more valuable practices such as taking care of their children. To emphasize the benefits that washing machines allow housewives to spend more time on leisure and self-improvements, the 1973 ad featured a picture of a woman knitting.

In 1974, Kumsung released another ad with an unconventional headline: "I will take over..." followed by a body copy Laundry is the most significant burden on our wives.[17] So far, it is not much different from the old ad, the following line

---

[17] Dongah Ilbo, 'I will take over … [내가 대신 …]'.1974 [Naver News Library]

"When seeing my wife struggling, I want to wash it for her." This advertising defied the assumption that housework is solely a female task by depicting it from the perspective of men who are willing to help with the duties. This example shows that the intended audience of "The Swan Laundry Machine" shifted from housewives to men. Although the users were women, men performed the decision-making and financial support that led to the actual purchase of these machines. With the rapid expansion of economic industrialization, industrial products such as the washing machine soon appeared as holiday gifts, and companies started advertising phrases that lulled husbands to buy "The Swan Laundry Machine" for their wives as holiday gifts.

Korea was in the midst of a social, cultural, and economic transformation in the 1970s, which resulted in significant changes in women's status, values, and social demands. It was an era in which women gained a new sense of self-awareness, allowing them to live their lives. In the 1970s following the Korean War, the economic participation of the baby boom generation increased, and the social status of women improved compared to the previous era. After the machine failed to succeed in its first appearance due to a lack of customer awareness and prejudice against housework, Kumsung redesigned the advertisements published in Dongah Ilbo. In existing advertising, the focus was on technology and instructions and there was little information to inform those new to washing machines about the machine's role and effectiveness. Later Kumsung Through a series of modifications in marketing strategies, Korean washing machines passed through the prenatal era (1699-1979), the growth period (1980-1989), and the functional diversifier era (1990-1999) through a series of marketing strategy changes to arrive at their current look.[18]

Diffusion of Washing Machine

When Korea's first washing machine appeared in the late 1960s, Japan's penetration rate in households was 70%. Until 1975, the number of households with washing machines was only 1%. It became 26% in 1985, and 55% in 1988,

---

[18] Mun, Hye Gyŏng. "set'akpangbŏbŭi pyŏnch'ŏn'gwa set'akki paldare kwanhan yŏn'gu." (1997): 1-70.

then 99.9% in 1997.[19] Penetration rate of washing machines increased by an average of 10% annually from the late 1970s to 1990s. The spread of washing machines in Korea was followed by the country's fast industrialization, which resulted in higher living standards and wages, as well as changes in women's social status. As Korea's industrialization progressed, the CPI increased from 7.3 in 1970 to 252.5 in 1993 (3,500%), and salaries increased in lockstep with the CPI: rising wages for housekeeping services and encouraging women to join in economic activities.[20] As wages rose, so did the demand for and growth of domestic labor mechanization.

Consequently, as wages increased, the number of employed housekeepers declined. With rising salaries, it became more expensive for families to employ housekeepers to help with household chores. At that time, the wage level of home employees jumped more than 10 times from 6,447 won in 1970 to 69,995 won in 1980. By the late 1970s it was cheaper to buy a laundry machine than to hire a housemaid. As the financial burden of hiring housekeepers increased, the proportion of household chores that housewives had to handle on their own increased. Initially, housekeepers were hired to perform the unpleasant laundry and cleaning chores. For those who didn't have access to a washing machine, doing the weekly wash was solely the responsibility of the housewife.

Due to an increased financial burden, the number of home makers employed within households dropped from 41.5% in 1970 to 14.3% in 1989. In 1989, the penetration rate of washing machines was more than 50% and 1% in 1975.[21] The decrease in domestic labor support incentivized households to search for alternatives to assist housework. Furthermore, as the minimum wage increased, females began to participate in economic activities increasing double income households. Higher economic activity among women resulted in increased income and time limitations, facilitating the development of home appliances. In Korea, the participation rate of women in economic activities Increased from 26.8% in 1960, to 40.6% in 1980.[22] Because of limited educational backgrounds,

---

[19] Lee, Ki Young. "The mechanization of Housework: Focused on Diffusion Process and influencing Factors". Kajŏnggwa Salmŭi Chil Yŏn'gu (2002): 70-80.

[20] Kim, Jŭng Hŭi. "han'guk chubuŭi kasanodongŭi kyŏngjejŏk kach'i p'yŏnggawa tae Gnp piyul ch'ujŏng." kajŏnghak sŏksa hagwinonmun (1994): 37-51.

[21] Lee, Ki Young. "The mechanization of Housework: Focused on Diffusion Process and influencing Factors". Kajŏnggwa Salmŭi Chil Yŏn'gu (2002): 70-80.

[22] Kim, Jŭng Hŭi. "han'guk chubuŭi kasanodongŭi kyŏngjejŏk kach'i p'yŏnggawa tae Gnp piyul ch'ujŏng." kajŏnghak sŏksa hagwinonmun (1994): 37-51.

most women worked in low-income jobs such as the agriculture and production industry, earning minimum wages. Therefore, the increase in employment of women did not significantly contribute to the increase in household income. Housewives, on the other hand, were plagued by time restraints. Females were compelled to work both within and outside the home, however they were understaffed to fulfill both tasks. As such, more low-income households started to consider laundry machines as a long-term investment.

Furthermore, there was an increase in purchasing power among households as males received greater minimum wages. As bottom-line incomes climbed, the cost of washing machines became less of a strain to obtain, allowing households to spend on items other than fundamental necessities. Laundry machines were considered relatively less expensive compared to the past, as they took up less of their total income. Between 1970 and 1990, when home appliances were widely distributed among households, total income increased by 20% annually from 185,000 won in 1970 to 724,000 won in 1990.[23] Indeed, from 1970 to 1990, wages increased 10 fold, while the price of washing machines increased 5 fold. Even with the increase in price, laundry machines became more affordable as disposable income increased. Thus, laundry machines, once considered luxury goods, now became a household necessity.[24] At the same time, the commodity tax on laundry machines was reduced, lowering the barriers of entry for laundry machines to diffuse into Korean households. With more disposable income, individuals were more willing to spend on products that filled beyond their basic needs.

Laundry could still be done by hand, but with fewer homemakers and higher household spending power, laundry machines grew in popularity. Housewives were able to ask and convey their demand for washers more comfortably without being considered irresponsible or demanding. As a result, the proportion spent on household appliances, accounted for total income, continued to increase from 1.0% in 1975 to 2.6% in 1980, 3.5% in 1985, and 5.4% in 1990.[25] Furthermore, the penetration rate of laundry machines together increased from 1% in the 1970s to 55% by 1988.[26] With the rapid industrialization in Korea, the demand for laundry machines increased and were able to penetrate deeply into Korea. Washing

---

[23] Mun, Hye Gyŏng. "set'akpangbŏbŭi pyŏnch'ŏn'gwa set'akki paldare kwanhan yŏn'gu." (1997): 1-70.

[24] *IBID.*

[25] *IBID.*

[26] *IBID.*

machines, which were considered luxury goods in Korea, gradually improved the standard of living for the people since the 1970s.

We looked at the introduction and proliferation of laundry machines throughout history. The situation in Korea prior to the introduction of the washing machine and how it spread throughout the country were addressed in the preceding section. The last section examines the impact of washing machines on Korea's current state since it became a necessity.

Laundry shaping domestic work

"Do you know what one of the biggest inventions of mankind is? It's the washing machine. The invention of the washing machine freed women from the time they struggled with the laundry and began to develop themselves at that time.", said Daniela Russ, director of the Artificial Intelligence Research Institute at the Massachusetts Institute of Technology (MIT). It was true that the electric washing machine made laundry less difficult and simplified the process. But did the work itself become less burdensome? Did the development of washing machines make women think of laundry as an enjoyable process?

The problem was that with rapid industrialization, personal hygiene and cleanliness standards have risen. Before industrialization, people didn't own many clothes, and they collected hard laundry at once and did it together, it wasn't done as often as nowadays.[27] Furthermore, women did not have to prepare business clothes such as shirts, which require frequent washing and ironing. Likewise, in the preparation of large laundries, such as bed sheets, expectations have developed that they must be washed frequently for sanitary reasons.[28] The process has been simplified by switching from handwashing to pushing buttons, however the frequency has increased, and the spectrum of laundry has widened.

The value and perception of household labor changed with the introduction of laundry machines. Unlike in the past, the impression that washing is difficult and should be assisted has gradually faded.[29] If housewives didn't complete domestic tasks, they were recognized as being lazy and were plagued by guilt that they were

---

[27] Chang, Unsu. "Set'akki Tŏkpune Kasanodong Haebang?… Ch'ŏnmane! ." Munhwailbo, 7 May 2020.

[28] *IBID.*

[29] *IBID.*

neglecting their families. [30] A home was described as a "refuge from the marginalized and stressed routine of work," and housework as "a housewife's expression of care for her family." [31] Before the introduction of the washing machine, domestic work was considered an essential labor that the whole family, including children, had to support and work together. With washers making the process easier, laundry began to be recognized as a trivial labor that could be easily completed and substituted with monetary values. Women's household labor was devalued and became "unpaid shadow labor". Cowan's "Strange Paradox" explains this well, taking a historical approach by looking into feminist movements and gender norms to explain why, despite the widespread usage of electricity and home appliances, time spent on housework has not decreased. Korea having a different industrialization timeline compared to the west, general idea could be applied but alteration of this model was required for further analysis. The agony of laundry was alleviated by the introduction of laundry machines, but as the frequency of washing rose, the overall time spent washing decreased by an insignificant amount. [32] This does not only apply to washing machines but also to other home appliances such as vacuum cleaners and refrigerators. [33] The mechanization of housework was a 'double-edged sword' for housewives.[34]

Women's housework hours have fallen noticeably by 20% since the 1990s, although the changes in overall hours spent have been negligible.[35] This was because men's participation rate in housework increased. As the mechanization of family work spread throughout Korea, it was an opportunity to remind us of a new time that housework, which was considered only a matter of course to be done, is a difficult task. Furthermore, feminist movement in Korea surged, as women's entry into society increased. What reduced women's housework was a movement that was initiated independently for women's rights as well as technology.

---

[30] *IBID.*

[31] Kim, Dukho. "Has Household Technology Lead to the Liberation of Domestic Labor?" Essay. In Betrayal of Laundry Machines, 251–87. ppuriwa ip'ari , 2020.

[32] Kim, Son Hui. "A Study on the Household Work Time's Change and Its Structure in Urban Home Makers." Journal of the Korean Home Economics Association(1989): 111-126.

[33] Kim, Dok Ho. "Home Appliances, Consumption Revolution, and the Making of the Mass Consumption Society in South Korea." Historical Criticism (2021): 269-300.

[34] *IBID.*

[35] *IBID.*

Conclusion

Korea has a distinct history of wearing white clothing. During the Three Kingdoms Period, commoners used to wear white garments due to societal restraints and later became a symbol of anti-Japanese sentiment during the Japanese colonial period. Nevertheless, even after the status system was abolished, some people continued to wear white clothes due to a shortage of dyeing supplies and procedures. With a long history of favoring white clothing, laundry grew in cultural significance. Homemakers sat by streams or rivers, had casual conversations with neighbors, recounted their daily lives, and sang to the sound of bats while doing their laundry. However, with the growth of water and sewage systems in the 1960s, laundry, which was previously done in a shared area, shifted to a highly private location.

As the primary location of laundry experienced a drastic shift, laundry became more privatized and was reclassified as 'work' rather than a social activity. Thus, the desire for mechanization of the laundry process soared among housewives and laundry machines started appearing in homes in 1970s Korea. Kumsung, the firm behind the first Korean Washing machine, made series of changes to their marketing strategy, namely by enforcing the need and making changes in the core message and targeted audience. As the public were unaware of laundry machine's potential, many households concluded that such devices were not worth paying double the monthly wage. As such, Kumsung modified their marketing strategy to stress the main advantage of using their washing machines. This campaign was directed at a variety of women living in various types of households, including newlyweds, apartment dwellers, double incomes, and large families. Later, with the introduction of nuclear families, advertising strategy was adjusted to target newlyweds and then to husbands.

With the increase in wages, it was no longer cost-efficient to hire housekeepers, females participated in workforce, and living standards increased. Washing machines increased women's time efficiency, but there was no significant change in the overall time spent on washing due to the overall raised personal living and hygienic standards. With the development of washing machines, the recognition of household labor by housewives decreased within the home, this surged the movement for women to independently regain their rights. The movement was an opportunity to awaken the value of women's housework, and induce the participation of men in household labor.